MASTERING MACHINE CODE ON YOUR COMMODORE 64

Mark Greenshields

This book is dedicated to my grandmother,
NANCY GREENSHIELDS

First Published in the United Kingdom
by Interface Publications

This Remastered Edition
Published in 2022 by
Acorn Books
acornbooks.uk

This book is a page-by-page reproduction of the original 1984 edition as published by Interface Publications. The entirety of the book is presented with no changes, corrections nor updates to the original text, images and layout; therefore no guarantee is offered as to the accuracy of the information within.

CONTENTS

SECTION 1

A complete listing of a 6510 assembler/dissassembler/ monitor.

A tutorial of every command in 6510 Assembly language and every programming mode of the 6510 chip, complete with examples throughout.

SECTION 2

This section of the book uses the knowledge acquired in Section 1 (and the assembler from the same) to show how scrolling (both pixel and character), Raster scan graphics and high resolution graphics may be produced via Assembly language.

It also shows how sound can be achieved properly in machine code.
You will learn how to use interrupts for doing things independently of the computer, eg. playing a tune through-out the running of a program without slowing it down, or while typing on the computer. There is a section on how to programme the function keys and how to simulate the ZX Spectrum keyboard (i.e. one key entry).

You will also be shown how to add commands to BASIC the easy way.

SECTION 3

All ROM routines are explained here, with instructions on their use.

APPENDICES

Memory map.

Colour, screen, ASCII charts, etc.

Kernal jump table listings.

6510 commands listed, along with their Hex and decimal equivalents.

SECTION 2 CONTENTS

PROGRAMS

ADDING COMMANDS TO BASIC

ACKNOWLEDGEMENTS

With thanks to my parents Jack and Sheila Greenshields, my sister Louise, my grandparents Roy and Gracie Reid, Douglas Grant, Ronnie Brown, Neil Kolban, Lesley Currie, Neil Dunlop, Mark Kelly, William Drummond, Graeme Douglas, Lynn Johnston, John Lovie, Jonathan Coggans, Lois Todd, Lesley Darling, Alan Fletcher, and all my relations for their encouragement.

Also, special thanks to COMMSCOT.

I would like to thank Jim Butterfield for his public domain program *SUPERMON*.

Finally, I would like to thank Liz North for all the encouragement that she has given me with the preparation of this book.

Mark Greenshields,
March 1984.

PREFACE

This book was not written just as a complete Assembly language tutorial on the Commodore 64. When I sat down to write this book I decided that there was no point in writing a book to teach Assembly language without including any practical routines that show how to make use of the language just learnt. Consequently, I wrote the second section to demonstrate how to use Assembly language to do things that everybody wants to do but cannot find any literature on how to do them. For example, scrolling, interrupts, Raster scan graphics and adding commands to BASIC.

The book is of use to both the beginner in Assembly language and advanced programmers who want to find out how to do more with their computer.

I hope you like the book and that it achieves what I had hoped when I wrote it.

Mark Greenshields
March 1984

INTRODUCTION

All the programs in this book were LISTed on a BMC Centronics printer. This printer cannot reproduce the standard Commodore symbols for colour controls, etc, so here is a list of the symbols and how they will appear in the listings.

```
{CLR}        IS CLEAR SCREEN
{HOME}       IS HOME CURSOR
{INST DEL}   IS INSERT
{BLK}        IS BLACK
{WHT}        IS WHITE
{RED}        IS RED
{CYN}        IS CYAN
{PUR}        IS PURPLE
{GRN}        IS GREEN
{BLU}        IS BLUE
{YEL}        IS YELLOW
{RVS ON}     IS RVS ON
{RVS OFF}    IS RVS OFF
{OR}         IS ORANGE
{BRN}        IS BROWN
{LT RED}     IS LIGHT RED
{GY 1}       IS GREY 1
{GY 2}       IS GREY 2
{LT GRN}     IS LIGHT GREEN
{LT BLU}     IS LIGHT BLUE
{GY 3}       IS GREY 3
{CUR DN}     IS CRSR DOWN
{CUR UP}     IS CRSR UP
{CUR RT}     IS CRSR RIGHT
{CUR L}      IS CRSR LEFT
```

SECTION ONE

SUPERMON

All the programs in this book are listed in mnemonic format and therefore need an assembler to enter them. This need not be a powerful macro-assembler, just a simple non-symbolic assembler will do.

Following is a listing of *SUPERMON* which is a public domain assembler/disassembler/monitor. Thanks to Jim Butterfield for this program. The BASIC program which precedes the data is used to enter this assembler. You will need this assembler or a similar one to enter all the programs in this book.

SUPERMON is listed as a Hex dump which is a listing of hexadecimal numbers. Using the BASIC loader program provided, you should find it easy to enter.

To enter *SUPERMON*, type in the following commands in direct mode (where '<return>' means press the Return key). Then type in the BASIC loader and SAVE it.

POKE 43,1 <return>
POKE 44,32 <return>
POKE 8192,0 <return>
NEW <return>

Now LOAD and RUN the loader and you should see the following prompt:

.0800?

You should note that the first number corresponds with the first number in the *SUPERMON* listing. This is an indication

1

that you should type in the data. To help you, the first three lines that you should type in are shown below. Type the program in without spaces.

```
.0800 ? 001A086400992293

.0808 ? 121D1D1D1D535550

.0810 ? 45522036342D4D4F
```

Don't worry if you don't understand what you are typing in. Just type exactly what is printed and it will work. All this initial hard work will be worth it in the end as writing machine code using an assembler is far easier than doing it by hand.

Once you have finished typing in the program you will be prompted with the message:

SAVE TO TAPE OR DISK?

Press 'T' if you are using cassette and have a blank cassette in the recorder. Press 'D' if you are using disk, and make sure that your disk is formatted with at least 11 blocks free.

If you pressed 'T' then you will be prompted with 'PRESS PLAY ON TAPE', and if you pressed 'D' the drive will start whirring. The program is now being SAVED to tape or disk. If an error occurs, then typing RUN100 will allow you to save the program again.

It can be loaded in the normal way, ie. LOAD"SUPER-MON",1 or LOAD"SUPERMON",8. Then you RUN the program and some writing will appear on the screen and a '.' prompt will appear. To make spare copies of SUPERMON just load the program and save it as if it was BASIC.

SUPERMON is given here as a relocatable loader in that it can be located anywhere in RAM. To adjust where it is to be located in memory, find the starting address and add 2065 to it. Now use the following formula to calculate the two numbers necessary.

LO=INT(number/256)
HI=((number/256)−LO)*256

Now POKE 55 with the value of LO and POKE 56 with the value of HI and RUN *SUPERMON*.

To re-start SUPERMON you should type 'SYS starting address+1'. (The normal value to start SUPERMON is SYS 38893.)

Here are the instructions for using *SUPERMON*. *SUPER-MON* commands are all one letter commands usually followed by parameters.

The first command that we will look at is 'A'. This stands for assemble and is the most frequently used command in any assembler. It will be used for entering almost all of the programs in this book.

The syntax for 'A' is as follows:

A (start address in Hex) (mnemonic) (operand)

eg. A 1000 LDA #$10

The address is the starting address in Hex. The mnemonic is the Assembly language command, and the operand is the number associated with the command if there is one.

After you press the Return key from the first line, if it is correct syntax the computer will prompt you with an 'A' and the next address. Therefore, you need only enter the starting address and the assembler does the rest. To leave the assembler, press the Return key.

Here is a simple example program. For now it is sufficient to see how the assembler works.

```
.A 1000 LDA #$00

.A 1002 STA $D020

.A 1005 STA $D021

.A 1008 RTS
```

The above program makes the screen and the border turn black. If you make an error, the computer will print a question mark. If this happens use the normal screen editor and change the mistake and delete the question mark. Press the Return key and if the next address is prompted, the line is now correct.

Now that you have typed this in you may want to SAVE the program. The command to do this is 'S'. The syntax is as follows:

S"name",device,start,end+1

The total length of the name must not exceed 16 characters or a question mark will be printed.

The 'device' is the device that the computer is to SAVE to 01 is tape and 08 is disk. The 0s before the number are essential for correct syntax.

The 'start' is the starting address in Hex of the SAVE.

The 'end+1' is the end address plus one that the computer is to save to. The reason that you must save up to the 'end+1' is that the ROM routine used to SAVE to memory saves up to, but not including, the end address specified. Note that all the parameters must be separated by a comma.

The next command is the command to execute a program in machine code from the assembler. It is 'G' and has the syntax:

G address to start at.

4

If you want to return control to the monitor when the program has been RUN, then make the last command of the program a BRK command instead of an RTS.

The Hex command allows you to see a program in memory.
It is 'D' and has the syntax:

D start

eg. D 1000

This command clears the screen and prints a page of commands. To see more press 'D' and the Return key.
The next command is the same as 'D', except that it prints a continuous listing without clearing the screen. The command is 'P' and it has the syntax:

P start end

It is mainly used when you want a printer listing. To print a disassembly to the printer, type the following in BASIC:

OPEN4,4 : CMD4 : SYS38893

(The SYS assumes that the monitor is at its default position in memory. If it isn't use your address.)

The printer will print something and then you can type what you want. You can use 'P' or 'M' (coming up next). To disable the printer when it has finished, type 'X' <return> (explained later) and CLOSE4. <return>.

Often you will want a listing of memory in Hex (like *SUPERMON*). This is done with the 'M' command which has the syntax:

M start end

Where 'start' and 'end' are in Hex. This command may also be used to the printer. (You may change memory using this command and then typing over values and pressing the Return key at the end of each line.)

The monitor has a command to fill areas of memory with a number. It is 'F' and it has the syntax:

F start end byte

Where 'start' and 'end' are addresses in Hex, and 'byte' is a byte in Hex.

SUPERMON has the facility to move parts of memory to another location. The command is 'T' which stands for Transfer memory. It has the syntax:

T oldstart oldend newstart

Where 'oldstart', 'oldend' and 'newstart' are addresses in Hex.

If you want to find the contents of the registers at any time, type the command 'R' on its own.

If you are working in the assembler and want to load a program into memory where it came from, there are two ways to do this: either return to BASIC and type LOAD "name", device,1 (eg. to load the file 'hello' from tape type LOAD"HELLO",1,1); or use the command 'L' in the monitor using the syntax . . . L"name", device (where 'device' is 01 for tape and 08 for disk).

To exit the assembler and return to BASIC, type 'X' <return> or press Run/Stop and Restore.

SUMMARY OF SUPERMON COMMANDS

COMMAND	MEANING	SYNTAX
A	Assemble mnemonics into memory	A 1000 LDA #$10
D	Disassemble memory	D 1000
M	Display Hex from memory	M 1000 2000
S	Save memory to device	S"name",08,1000,2000
L	Load memory from device	L"name",01
P	Print disassembly of memory	P 1000 2000
F	Fill memory	F 3000 4000 FF
T	Transfer memory to memory	T 1000 2000 C000
X	Exit to BASIC	X
R	Register display	R
G	Go to address	G FFD2

```
1 HE$="0123456789ABCDEF"
10 PRINT"{CLR}"
20 FORA=2049TO4587STEP8
30 GOSUB1000:REM CONVERT ADDRESS TO HEX
IN H$
40 PRINT".";H$;:INPUT A$:REM 8 HEX NUMBE
RS
50 FORX=1TO16STEP2
60 B$=MID$(A$,X,2)
70 GOSUB2000:REM CONVERT HEX NO. TO DECI
MAL
80 POKEA+X/2,HEX
90 NEXT:NEXT
100 INPUT"SAVE TO TAPE OR DISK";TD$
110 IFTD$="D"ORTD$="T"THEN120
115 GOTO100
120 IFTD$="D"THENDEV=8
130 IFTD$="T"THENDEV=1
140 FORA=0TO34:READB:POKEA+49152,B:NEXT:
POKE49153,DEV:INPUT"ARE YOU SURE";S$
```

7

```
150 IFS$="N"THEN100
160 SYS49152: REM SAVE ASSEMBLER
170 PRINT"MACHINE CODE SAVED"
180 PRINT"IT MAY BE LOADED FROM TAPE OR
DISK IN THE NORMAL WAY LIKE A BASIC"
190 PRINT"PROGRAM AND THEN RUN"
200 END
1000 N1=INT(A/4096):N6=(A/4096-N1)*16:N2
=INT(N6):N3=INT((N6-N2)*16)
1010 N4=(((N6-N2)*16)-N3)*16
1030 H$=MID$(HE$,N1+1,1)+MID$(HE$,N2+1,1
)+MID$(HE$,N3+1,1)+MID$(HE$,N4+1,1)
1040 RETURN
2000 FORV=1TO16:B=V-1:IFLEFT$(B$,1)=MID$
(HE$,V,1)THEN2020
2010 NEXT
2020 HEX=B*16
2030 FORV=1TO16:B=V-1:IFRIGHT$(B$,1)=MID
$(HE$,V,1)THEN2050
2040 NEXT
2050 HEX=HEX+B
2060 PRINT HEX
2070 RETURN
10000 DATA 162,1,160,1,32,186,255,162,26
,160,192,169,8,32,189,255,162,236,160
10010 DATA 17,169,251,32,216,255,96,83,8
5,80,69,82,77,79,78,0
.:0800 00 1A 08 64 00 99 22 93
.:0808 12 1D 1D 1D 1D 53 55 50
.:0810 45 52 20 36 34 2D 4D 4F
.:0818 4E 00 31 08 6E 00 99 22
.:0820 11 20 20 20 20 20 20 20
.:0828 20 20 20 20 20 20 20 20
.:0830 00 4B 08 78 00 99 22 11
.:0838 20 2E 2E 4A 49 4D 20 42
.:0840 55 54 54 45 52 46 49 45
.:0848 4C 44 00 66 08 82 00 9E
.:0850 28 C2 28 34 33 29 AA 32
.:0858 35 36 AC C2 28 34 34 29
.:0860 AA 31 32 37 29 00 00 00
```

```
.:0868  AA AA AA AA AA AA AA AA
.:0870  AA AA AA AA AA AA AA AA
.:0878  AA AA AA AA AA AA AA AA
.:0880  A5 2D 85 22 A5 2E 85 23
.:0888  A5 37 85 24 A5 38 85 25
.:0890  A0 00 A5 22 D0 02 C6 23
.:0898  C6 22 B1 22 D0 3C A5 22
.:08A0  D0 02 C6 23 C6 22 B1 22
.:08A8  F0 21 85 26 A5 22 D0 02
.:08B0  C6 23 C6 22 B1 22 18 65
.:08B8  24 AA A5 26 65 25 48 A5
.:08C0  37 D0 02 C6 38 C6 37 68
.:08C8  91 37 8A 48 A5 37 D0 02
.:08D0  C6 38 C6 37 68 91 37 18
.:08D8  90 B6 C9 4F D0 ED A5 37
.:08E0  85 33 A5 38 85 34 6C 37
.:08E8  00 4F 4F 4F 4F AD E6 FF
.:08F0  00 8D 16 03 AD E7 FF 00
.:08F8  8D 17 03 A9 80 20 90 FF
.:0900  00 00 D8 68 8D 3E 02 68
.:0908  8D 3D 02 68 8D 3C 02 68
.:0910  8D 3B 02 68 AA 68 A8 38
.:0918  8A E9 02 8D 3A 02 98 E9
.:0920  00 00 8D 39 02 BA 8E 3F
.:0928  02 20 57 FD 00 A2 42 A9
.:0930  2A 20 57 FA 00 A9 52 D0
.:0938  34 E6 C1 D0 06 E6 C2 D0
.:0940  02 E6 26 60 20 CF FF C9
.:0948  0D D0 F8 68 68 EA EA EA
.:0950  EA EA A9 00 00 85 26 A2
.:0958  0D A9 2E 20 57 FA 00 EA
.:0960  EA EA EA EA 20 3E F8 00
.:0968  C9 2E F0 F9 C9 20 F0 F5
.:0970  A2 0E DD B7 FF 00 D0 0C
.:0978  8A 0A AA BD C7 FF 00 48
.:0980  BD C6 FF 00 48 60 CA 10
.:0988  EC 4C ED FA 00 A5 C1 8D
.:0990  3A 02 A5 C2 8D 39 02 60
.:0998  A9 08 85 1D A0 00 00 20
.:09A0  54 FD 00 B1 C1 20 48 FA
```

9

```
.:Ø9A8 ØØ 2Ø 33 F8 ØØ C6 1D DØ
.:Ø9BØ F1 6Ø 2Ø 88 FA ØØ 9Ø ØB
.:Ø9B8 A2 ØØ ØØ 81 C1 C1 C1 FØ
.:Ø9CØ Ø3 4C ED FA ØØ 2Ø 33 F8
.:Ø9C8 ØØ C6 1D 6Ø A9 3B 85 C1
.:Ø9DØ A9 Ø2 85 C2 A9 Ø5 6Ø 98
.:Ø9D8 48 2Ø 57 FD ØØ 68 A2 2E
.:Ø9EØ 4C 57 FA ØØ EA EA EA EA
.:Ø9E8 EA A2 ØØ ØØ BD EA FF ØØ
.:Ø9FØ 2Ø D2 FF E8 EØ 16 DØ F5
.:Ø9F8 AØ 3B 2Ø C2 F8 ØØ AD 39
.:ØAØØ Ø2 2Ø 48 FA ØØ AD 3A Ø2
.:ØAØ8 2Ø 48 FA ØØ 2Ø B7 F8 ØØ
.:ØA1Ø 2Ø 8D F8 ØØ FØ 5C 2Ø 3E
.:ØA18 F8 ØØ 2Ø 79 FA ØØ 9Ø 33
.:ØA2Ø 2Ø 69 FA ØØ 2Ø 3E F8 ØØ
.:ØA28 2Ø 79 FA ØØ 9Ø 28 2Ø 69
.:ØA3Ø FA ØØ EA EA EA EA EA 2Ø
.:ØA38 E1 FF FØ 3C A6 26 DØ 38
.:ØA4Ø A5 C3 C5 C1 A5 C4 E5 C2
.:ØA48 9Ø 2E AØ 3A 2Ø C2 F8 ØØ
.:ØA5Ø 2Ø 41 FA ØØ 2Ø 8B F8 ØØ
.:ØA58 FØ EØ 4C ED FA ØØ 2Ø 79
.:ØA6Ø FA ØØ 9Ø Ø3 2Ø 8Ø F8 ØØ
.:ØA68 2Ø B7 F8 ØØ DØ Ø7 2Ø 79
.:ØA7Ø FA ØØ 9Ø EB A9 Ø8 85 1D
.:ØA78 2Ø 3E F8 ØØ 2Ø A1 F8 ØØ
.:ØA8Ø DØ F8 4C 47 F8 ØØ 2Ø CF
.:ØA88 FF C9 ØD FØ ØC C9 2Ø DØ
.:ØA9Ø D1 2Ø 79 FA ØØ 9Ø Ø3 2Ø
.:ØA98 8Ø F8 ØØ EA EA EA EA EA
.:ØAAØ AE 3F Ø2 9A 78 AD 39 Ø2
.:ØAA8 48 AD 3A Ø2 48 AD 3B Ø2
.:ØABØ 48 AD 3C Ø2 AE 3D Ø2 AC
.:ØAB8 3E Ø2 4Ø EA EA EA EA EA
.:ØACØ AE 3F Ø2 9A 6C Ø2 AØ AØ
.:ØAC8 Ø1 84 BA 84 B9 88 84 B7
.:ØADØ 84 9Ø 84 93 A9 4Ø 85 BB
.:ØAD8 A9 Ø2 85 BC 2Ø CF FF C9
.:ØAEØ 2Ø FØ F9 C9 ØD FØ 38 C9
```

```
.:ØAE8 22 DØ 14 2Ø CF FF C9 22
.:ØAFØ FØ 1Ø C9 ØD FØ 29 91 BB
.:ØAF8 E6 B7 C8 CØ 1Ø DØ EC 4C
.:ØBØØ ED FA ØØ 2Ø CF FF C9 ØD
.:ØBØ8 FØ 16 C9 2C DØ DC 2Ø 88
.:ØB1Ø FA ØØ 29 ØF FØ E9 C9 Ø3
.:ØB18 FØ E5 85 BA 2Ø CF FF C9
.:ØB2Ø ØD 6Ø 6C 3Ø Ø3 6C 32 Ø3
.:ØB28 2Ø 96 F9 ØØ DØ D4 EA EA
.:ØB3Ø EA EA EA A9 ØØ ØØ 2Ø EF
.:ØB38 F9 ØØ A5 9Ø 29 1Ø DØ C4
.:ØB4Ø 4C 47 F8 ØØ 2Ø 96 F9 ØØ
.:ØB48 C9 2C DØ BA 2Ø 79 FA ØØ
.:ØB5Ø 2Ø 69 FA ØØ 2Ø CF FF C9
.:ØB58 2C DØ AD 2Ø 79 FA ØØ A5
.:ØB6Ø C1 85 AE A5 C2 85 AF 2Ø
.:ØB68 69 FA ØØ 2Ø CF FF C9 ØD
.:ØB7Ø DØ 98 EA EA EA EA EA 2Ø
.:ØB78 F2 F9 ØØ 4C 47 F8 ØØ A5
.:ØB8Ø C2 2Ø 48 FA ØØ A5 C1 48
.:ØB88 4A 4A 4A 4A 2Ø 6Ø FA ØØ
.:ØB9Ø AA 68 29 ØF 2Ø 6Ø FA ØØ
.:ØB98 48 8A 2Ø D2 FF 68 4C D2
.:ØBAØ FF Ø9 3Ø C9 3A 9Ø Ø2 69
.:ØBA8 Ø6 6Ø A2 Ø2 B5 CØ 48 B5
.:ØBBØ C2 95 CØ 68 95 C2 CA DØ
.:ØBB8 F3 6Ø 2Ø 88 FA ØØ 9Ø Ø2
.:ØBCØ 85 C2 2Ø 88 FA ØØ 9Ø Ø2
.:ØBC8 85 C1 6Ø A9 ØØ ØØ 85 2A
.:ØBDØ 2Ø 3E F8 ØØ C9 2Ø DØ Ø9
.:ØBD8 2Ø 3E F8 ØØ C9 2Ø DØ ØE
.:ØBEØ 18 6Ø 2Ø AF FA ØØ ØA ØA
.:ØBE8 ØA ØA 85 2A 2Ø 3E F8 ØØ
.:ØBFØ 2Ø AF FA ØØ Ø5 2A 38 6Ø
.:ØBF8 C9 3A 9Ø Ø2 69 Ø8 29 ØF
.:ØCØØ 6Ø A2 Ø2 2C A2 ØØ ØØ B4
.:ØCØ8 C1 DØ Ø8 B4 C2 DØ Ø2 E6
.:ØC1Ø 26 D6 C2 D6 C1 6Ø 2Ø 3E
.:ØC18 F8 ØØ C9 2Ø FØ F9 6Ø A9
.:ØC2Ø ØØ ØØ 8D ØØ ØØ Ø1 2Ø CC
```

```
.:0C28 FA 00 20 8F FA 00 20 7C
.:0C30 FA 00 90 09 60 20 3E F8
.:0C38 00 20 79 FA 00 B0 DE AE
.:0C40 3F 02 9A EA EA EA EA EA
.:0C48 A9 3F 20 D2 FF 4C 47 F8
.:0C50 00 20 54 FD 00 CA D0 FA
.:0C58 60 E6 C3 D0 02 E6 C4 60
.:0C60 A2 02 B5 C0 48 B5 27 95
.:0C68 C0 68 95 27 CA D0 F3 60
.:0C70 A5 C3 A4 C4 38 E9 02 B0
.:0C78 0E 88 90 0B A5 28 A4 29
.:0C80 4C 33 FB 00 A5 C3 A4 C4
.:0C88 38 E5 C1 85 1E 98 E5 C2
.:0C90 A8 05 1E 60 20 D4 FA 00
.:0C98 20 69 FA 00 20 E5 FA 00
.:0CA0 20 0C FB 00 20 E5 FA 00
.:0CA8 20 2F FB 00 20 69 FA 00
.:0CB0 90 15 A6 26 D0 64 20 28
.:0CB8 FB 00 90 5F A1 C1 81 C3
.:0CC0 20 05 FB 00 20 33 F8 00
.:0CC8 D0 EB 20 28 FB 00 18 A5
.:0CD0 1E 65 C3 85 C3 98 65 C4
.:0CD8 85 C4 20 0C FB 00 A6 26
.:0CE0 D0 3D A1 C1 81 C3 20 28
.:0CE8 FB 00 B0 34 20 B8 FA 00
.:0CF0 20 BB FA 00 4C 7D FB 00
.:0CF8 20 D4 FA 00 20 69 FA 00
.:0D00 20 E5 FA 00 20 69 FA 00
.:0D08 20 3E F8 00 20 88 FA 00
.:0D10 90 14 85 1D A6 26 D0 11
.:0D18 20 2F FB 00 90 0C A5 1D
.:0D20 81 C1 20 33 F8 00 D0 EE
.:0D28 4C ED FA 00 4C 47 F8 00
.:0D30 20 D4 FA 00 20 69 FA 00
.:0D38 20 E5 FA 00 20 69 FA 00
.:0D40 20 3E F8 00 A2 00 00 20
.:0D48 3E F8 00 C9 27 D0 14 20
.:0D50 3E F8 00 9D 10 02 E8 20
.:0D58 CF FF C9 0D F0 22 E0 20
.:0D60 D0 F1 F0 1C 8E 00 00 01
```

```
.:0D68 20 8F FA 00 90 C6 9D 10
.:0D70 02 E8 20 CF FF C9 0D F0
.:0D78 09 20 88 FA 00 90 B6 E0
.:0D80 20 D0 EC 86 1C A9 90 20
.:0D88 D2 FF 20 57 FD 00 A2 00
.:0D90 00 A0 00 00 B1 C1 DD 10
.:0D98 02 D0 0C C8 E8 E4 1C D0
.:0DA0 F3 20 41 FA 00 20 54 FD
.:0DA8 00 20 33 F8 00 A6 26 D0
.:0DB0 8D 20 2F FB 00 B0 DD 4C
.:0DB8 47 F8 00 20 D4 FA 00 85
.:0DC0 20 A5 C2 85 21 A2 00 00
.:0DC8 86 28 A9 93 20 D2 FF EA
.:0DD0 EA EA EA EA A9 16 85 1D
.:0DD8 20 6A FC 00 20 CA FC 00
.:0DE0 85 C1 84 C2 C6 1D D0 F2
.:0DE8 A9 91 20 D2 FF 4C 47 F8
.:0DF0 00 A0 2C 20 C2 F8 00 20
.:0DF8 54 FD 00 20 41 FA 00 20
.:0E00 54 FD 00 A2 00 00 A1 C1
.:0E08 20 D9 FC 00 48 20 1F FD
.:0E10 00 68 20 35 FD 00 A2 06
.:0E18 E0 03 D0 12 A4 1F F0 0E
.:0E20 A5 2A C9 E8 B1 C1 B0 1C
.:0E28 20 C2 FC 00 88 D0 F2 06
.:0E30 2A 90 0E BD 2A FF 00 20
.:0E38 A5 FD 00 BD 30 FF 00 F0
.:0E40 03 20 A5 FD 00 CA D0 D5
.:0E48 60 20 CD FC 00 AA E8 D0
.:0E50 01 C8 98 20 C2 FC 00 8A
.:0E58 86 1C 20 48 FA 00 A6 1C
.:0E60 60 A5 1F 38 A4 C2 AA 10
.:0E68 01 88 65 C1 90 01 C8 60
.:0E70 A8 4A 90 0B 4A B0 17 C9
.:0E78 22 F0 13 29 07 09 80 4A
.:0E80 AA BD D9 FE 00 B0 04 4A
.:0E88 4A 4A 4A 29 0F D0 04 A0
.:0E90 80 A9 00 00 AA BD 1D FF
.:0E98 00 85 2A 29 03 85 1F 98
.:0EA0 29 8F AA 98 A0 03 E0 8A
```

```
.:0EA8 F0 0B 4A 90 08 4A 4A 09
.:0EB0 20 88 D0 FA C8 88 D0 F2
.:0EB8 60 B1 C1 20 C2 FC 00 A2
.:0EC0 01 20 FE FA 00 C4 1F C8
.:0EC8 90 F1 A2 03 C0 04 90 F2
.:0ED0 60 A8 B9 37 FF 00 85 28
.:0ED8 B9 77 FF 00 85 29 A9 00
.:0EE0 00 A0 05 06 29 26 28 2A
.:0EE8 88 D0 F8 69 3F 20 D2 FF
.:0EF0 CA D0 EC A9 20 2C A9 0D
.:0EF8 4C D2 FF 20 D4 FA 00 20
.:0F00 69 FA 00 20 E5 FA 00 20
.:0F08 69 FA 00 A2 00 00 86 28
.:0F10 EA EA EA EA EA 20 57 FD
.:0F18 00 20 72 FC 00 20 CA FC
.:0F20 00 85 C1 84 C2 20 E1 FF
.:0F28 F0 05 20 2F FB 00 B0 E9
.:0F30 4C 47 F8 00 20 D4 FA 00
.:0F38 A9 03 85 1D 20 3E F8 00
.:0F40 20 A1 F8 00 D0 F8 A5 20
.:0F48 85 C1 A5 21 85 C2 4C 46
.:0F50 FC 00 C5 28 F0 03 20 D2
.:0F58 FF 60 20 D4 FA 00 20 69
.:0F60 FA 00 8E 11 02 A2 03 20
.:0F68 CC FA 00 48 CA D0 F9 A2
.:0F70 03 68 38 E9 3F A0 05 4A
.:0F78 6E 11 02 6E 10 02 88 D0
.:0F80 F6 CA D0 ED A2 02 20 CF
.:0F88 FF C9 0D F0 1E C9 20 F0
.:0F90 F5 20 D0 FE 00 B0 0F 20
.:0F98 9C FA 00 A4 C1 84 C2 85
.:0FA0 C1 A9 30 9D 10 02 E8 9D
.:0FA8 10 02 E8 D0 DB 86 28 A2
.:0FB0 00 00 86 26 F0 04 E6 26
.:0FB8 F0 75 A2 00 00 86 1D A5
.:0FC0 26 20 D9 FC 00 A6 2A 86
.:0FC8 29 AA BC 37 FF 00 BD 77
.:0FD0 FF 00 20 B9 FE 00 D0 E3
.:0FD8 A2 06 E0 03 D0 19 A4 1F
.:0FE0 F0 15 A5 2A C9 E8 A9 30
```

```
.:0FE8 B0 21 20 BF FE 00 D0 CC
.:0FF0 20 C1 FE 00 D0 C7 88 D0
.:0FF8 EB 06 2A 90 0B BC 30 FF
.:1000 00 BD 2A FF 00 20 B9 FE
.:1008 00 D0 B5 CA D0 D1 F0 0A
.:1010 20 B8 FE 00 D0 AB 20 B8
.:1018 FE 00 D0 A6 A5 28 C5 1D
.:1020 D0 A0 20 69 FA 00 A4 1F
.:1028 F0 28 A5 29 C9 9D D0 1A
.:1030 20 1C FB 00 90 0A 98 D0
.:1038 04 A5 1E 10 0A 4C ED FA
.:1040 00 C8 D0 FA A5 1E 10 F6
.:1048 A4 1F D0 03 B9 C2 00 00
.:1050 91 C1 88 D0 F8 A5 26 91
.:1058 C1 20 CA FC 00 85 C1 84
.:1060 C2 EA EA EA EA EA A0 41
.:1068 20 C2 F8 00 20 54 FD 00
.:1070 20 41 FA 00 20 54 FD 00
.:1078 EA EA EA EA EA 4C B0 FD
.:1080 00 A8 20 BF FE 00 D0 11
.:1088 98 F0 0E 86 1C A6 1D DD
.:1090 10 02 08 E8 86 1D A6 1C
.:1098 28 60 C9 30 90 03 C9 47
.:10A0 60 38 60 40 02 45 03 D0
.:10A8 08 40 09 30 22 45 33 D0
.:10B0 08 40 09 40 02 45 33 D0
.:10B8 08 40 09 40 02 45 B3 D0
.:10C0 08 40 09 00 00 22 44 33
.:10C8 D0 8C 44 00 00 11 22 44
.:10D0 33 D0 8C 44 9A 10 22 44
.:10D8 33 D0 08 40 09 10 22 44
.:10E0 33 D0 08 40 09 62 13 78
.:10E8 A9 00 00 21 81 82 00 00
.:10F0 00 00 59 4D 91 92 86 4A
.:10F8 85 9D 2C 29 2C 23 28 24
.:1100 59 00 00 58 24 24 00 00
.:1108 1C 8A 1C 23 5D 8B 1B A1
.:1110 9D 8A 1D 23 9D 8B 1D A1
.:1118 00 00 29 19 AE 69 A8 19
.:1120 23 24 53 1B 23 24 53 19
```

15

```
.:1128 A1 00 00 1A 5B 5B A5 69
.:1130 24 24 AE AE A8 AD 29 00
.:1138 00 7C 00 00 15 9C 6D 9C
.:1140 A5 69 29 53 84 13 34 11
.:1148 A5 69 23 A0 D8 62 5A 48
.:1150 26 62 94 88 54 44 C8 54
.:1158 68 44 E8 94 00 00 B4 08
.:1160 84 74 B4 28 6E 74 F4 CC
.:1168 4A 72 F2 A4 8A 00 00 AA
.:1170 A2 A2 74 74 74 72 44 68
.:1178 B2 32 B2 00 00 22 00 00
.:1180 1A 1A 26 26 72 72 88 C8
.:1188 C4 CA 26 48 44 44 A2 C8
.:1190 3A 3B 52 4D 47 58 4C 53
.:1198 54 46 48 44 50 2C 41 42
.:11A0 F9 00 35 F9 00 CC F8 00
.:11A8 F7 F8 00 56 F9 00 89 F9
.:11B0 00 F4 F9 00 0C FA 00 3E
.:11B8 FB 00 92 FB 00 C0 FB 00
.:11C0 38 FC 00 5B FD 00 8A FD
.:11C8 00 AC FD 00 46 F8 00 FF
.:11D0 F7 00 ED F7 00 0D 20 20
.:11D8 20 50 43 20 20 53 52 20
.:11E0 41 43 20 58 52 20 59 52
.:11E8 20 53 50 00 00 00 00 00
```

NUMBERING SYSTEMS

There are three numbering systems used in the 6510 processor.

1: HEXADECIMAL

This is the most common numbering system employed on the 6510. It is similar to decimal except that the numbers are made up of multiples of 16 digits instead of 10. It is therefore referred to as a base 16 numbering system.

A decimal number has a base of 10 (therefore, it has 10 digits which are combined to make up any number—these are the numerals '0' to '9'). In Hex we need 16 digits as it is a base 16 numbering system, so the first six letters of the alphabet are used to represent the numbers 10 to 15 (A–F).

DECIMAL	HEXADECIMAL
0	00
1	01
2	02
3	03
4	04
5	05
6	06
7	07
8	08
9	09
10	0A
11	0B
12	0C
13	0D
14	0E
15	0F
16	10
17	11

And so on. . .

17

In decimal as you move left along a number the powers of 10 increase by one each time. For example, '9454' is (9*1000)+(4*100)+(5*10)+(4). In hexadecimal (Hex), it is the powers of 16 that increase by one each time. For example, '1ED2' is (1*4096)+(14*256)+(13*16)+(2). It is also worth noting that the range of numbers that we can use in decimal are from zero to 65535 inclusive whereas in Hex the range is from 0000 to FFFF.

2: BINARY

Binary numbers are base two and therefore need only two digits—these are one and zero (1,0). As you move left along the table shown below, the powers of two increase by one each time.

128 64 32 16 8 4 2 1

 1   0   0   1 1 1 1 0

The above number in binary (10011110) is 128+16+8+4+2 (158) in decimal.

3: BINARY CODED DECIMAL

Binary coded decimal is a numbering system unique to the 6500 series of microprocessors. It is used where decimal output is required as it makes hexadecimal numbers behave like decimal. This will all be explained at a later stage (see SED, CLD).

6510 ASSEMBLY LANGUAGE TUTORIAL

Machine code is not as difficult to learn as a first glance would make you think. Although it seems far more complex than BASIC, once you grasp the principles it is all fairly straightforward. Interested? Well, let's get underway.

All the routines in this book should be typed into the computer using an assembler. If you don't have one then use *SUPERMON*.

You may now be asking "What is machine code?". Well quite simply, it is the language that the microprocessor in your CBM 64 understands. How then can you write programs in BASIC? The BASIC language is actually a huge machine language program that interprets (changes) the BASIC commands into machine code for the computer to execute. The CBM 64 has a 6510 microprocessor (an upgraded 6502), so it understands 6510 machine code.

Let us compare a simple program in BASIC and then its machine code equivalent.

```
10 A=1:B=1
20 C=A+B
30 PRINT C
40 END
```

That's pretty straightforward, isn't it—here is the 6510 machine code equivalent.

A9 01 69 0A 8D 00 04 A9 01 8D 00 D8 60

All rather unintelligible to the uninitiated. Because this is so difficult to read there is a human version of machine code

19

called Assembly language. Here is the above program in Assembly language.

```
LDA #$01    :A=1
ADC #$01    :Add one
STA $0400   :PRINT result
LDA #$01    :Make character appear
STA $d800   :in white
RTS         :End
```

This is much easier to understand. Assembly language is made up of 56 three letter 'words' which are used in various ways called addressing modes.

Here is an explanation of the seven addressing modes. They will be explained more fully as we go on.

1. **Immediate addressing:** Directly doing something without accessing memory.

2. **Absolute addressing:** Accessing memory locations while doing something.

3. **Zero Page addressing:** Accessing memory while doing something, but only in the range zero to 255.

4. **Indexed addressing:** Accessing memory with an offset from the 'X' or 'Y' registers.

5. **Implied addressing:** Jumping to a location through two others. Used only with the 'JMP' command.

6. **Indirect Indexed addressing:** Accessing memory through two other registers plus an offset.

7. **Indexed Indirect addressing:** Accessing memory through two other registers plus an offset (different to (6)).

6510 Instruction Set

LDA	Loads the Accumulator with memory or a number.
LDX	Loads the 'X' register with memory or a number.
LDY	Loads the 'Y' register with memory or a number.
STA	Stores a number in the Accumulator in memory location.
STX	Stores a number in the 'X' register in memory location.
STY	Stores a number in the 'Y' register in memory location.
TAX	Transfers the contents of the Accumulator into the 'X' register.
TAY	Transfers the contents of the Accumulator into the 'Y' register.
TXA	Transfers the contents of the 'X' register into the Accumulator.
TYA	Transfers the contents of the 'Y' register into the Accumulator.
NOP	No operation (used to fill memory).
JMP	Jumps to address. . .
JSR	Jumps to a subroutine at address. . .
RTS	Returns from a subroutine or to BASIC.
INC	Increments (add one to) memory.
INX	Increments the value in 'X'.
INY	Increments the value in 'Y'.
DEC	Decrements (subtract one from) memory.

DEX	Decrements the value in 'X'.
DEY	Decrements the value in 'Y'.
CMP	Compares 'A' with memory/number.
CPX	Compares 'X' with memory/number.
CPY	Compares 'Y' with memory/number.
BEQ	Branches if value equal to zero.
BNE	Branches if value not equal to zero.
BCC	Branches if carry clear (less than).
BCS	Branches if carry set (more than).
BVC	Branches if overflow.
BVS	Branches if no overflow.
BPL	Branches on plus (less than 128).
BMI	Branches on minus (more than 128).
BRK	Forces a stop in the program.
PHA	Puts the value in A on to the top of the stack.
PHP	Puts the processor status on to the stack.
PLA	Takes the value off the top of the stack and puts it in 'A'.
PLP	Takes the status off the top of the stack and puts it in the status register.
TXS	Transfers the value in 'X' to the stack pointer.
TSX	Transfers the stack pointer to 'X'.
AND	AND 'A' with memory or a number.
ORA	OR 'A' with memory or a number.
EOR	Exclusive OR 'A' with memory or a number.
BIT	AND 'A' with memory or a number, but leave 'A' and the memory intact changing only the flags.

ADC	Adds memory or a number to 'A' with carry.
SBC	Subtracts memory or a number from 'A' with carry.
SEC	Sets carry.
CLC	Clears carry.
SED	Sets decimal mode (BCD).
CLD	Clears decimal mode.
SEI	Sets interrupt disable.
CLI	Clears interrupt disable.
RTI	Returns from interrupt.
CLV	Sets the overflow bit.
ROR	Rotates memory one bit right.
ROL	Rotates memory one bit left.
ASL	Shifts memory one bit left.
LSR	Shifts memory one bit right.

We will start with the command 'LDA'. This means LoaD (or fill) the Accumulator with a value, or a value from an address.

eg. LDA #$10 : Put the value 10 (Hex because of the $ sign) into the Accumulator.

Once you have loaded a value in the Accumulator, you may want to do something with it. The command 'STA' puts the value in 'A' into a memory location. This is equivalent to the BASIC command 'POKE'.

eg. LDA #$01 : This puts an 'A' in the top left area of the screen.

STA $0400

We can also load the Accumulator with values from memory locations. There are various formats for this:

23

LDA $address : Where 'address' is between zero and 255.
LDA $address : Where 'address' is between zero and 65535.

   We can also use the 'X' and 'Y' registers for the same purpose:

LDX #$0A   : Load 'X' with 0A (Hex).
LDX $address : Load 'X' with a value in an address, where 'address' is between zero and 255.
LDX $address : Load 'X' with a value in an address, where 'address' is between zero and 65535.
LDY #$06   : Load 'Y' with 06 (Hex).
LDY $address : Load 'Y' with a value in an address, where 'address' is between zero and 255.
LDY $address : Load 'Y' with a value in an address, where 'address' is between zero and 65535.
STX $address : Store a value in 'X' in an address, where 'address' is between zero and 255.
STX $address : Store a value in 'X' in an address, where 'address' is between zero and 65535.
STY $address : Store a value in 'Y' in an address, where 'address' is between zero and 255.
STY $address : Store a value in 'Y' in an address, where 'address' is between zero and 65535.

Values can easily be transferred between registers. There are commands within the 6510 to do this and they are as follows:

TAX : Transfers the contents of 'A' to 'X' leaving 'A' the same. (If 'A' contains '12' and you use the TAX command, both 'A' and 'X' will contain the value 12.)
TAY : Transfers the contents of 'A' to 'Y' leaving 'A' the same.
TXA : Transfers the contents of 'X' to 'A' leaving 'X' the same.
TYA : Transfers the contents of 'Y' to 'A' leaving 'Y' the same.

Assemblers that do not allow the use of labels (as in the one at the beginning of the book) need some way of reserving space in the middle of your program in case you want to insert or extend a routine. There is a command for the 6510 that does just that—it acts just like 'REM' in BASIC, in that the processor totally ignores it and goes on to the next instruction. This command is 'NOP' and it stands by itself.

In a program you may want to jump to another part of the program just as you would GOTO in BASIC. The command to do this is 'JMP address'. For example, to jump to address 3F00 (Hex) the command is JMP $3F00. You may also wish to jump to a subroutine as you would GOSUB in BASIC. The command for this is 'JSR address'—to jump to a subroutine starting at $4000 the command would be JSR $4000.

There will come a time when you want to return to the main program from the subroutine. The command to do this is 'RTS' which does exactly the same as RETURN does in BASIC. If you have not JSR'd to a routine or returned from it, the 'RTS' command will also return control to BASIC.

Now let's put some of the above commands to work. If you have typed in the *SUPERMON* assembler or have a similar one already, then type in the following program.

First enter the assembler with 'SYS 38893' (or however you enter your own assembler) then type the following:

```
.A 4000 LDA #$00   : Load the Accumulator with zero.
.A 4002 STA $D020  : Put it in $D020 (53280 dec)
.A 4005 STA $D021  : Put it in $D021 (53281 dec)
.A 4008 RTS        : Return to BASIC.
```

To start this program type 'G 4000'. The screen and border will now turn black. You have now entered your first machine code program. You may say "But that's Assembly language, not machine code". You are wrong. . .you typed Assembly language into the computer, but the assembler transformed it into machine code. To see this machine code,

25

type 'M 4000 4009'. You should see the following on the screen:

```
M 4000 4008
.;4000 A9 00 8D 20 D0 8D 21 D0
.;4008 60 00 00 00 00 00 00 00
```

The numbers in the second row after the '60' may differ but don't worry, the program ends at the 60 (RTS).

Here is a program that uses all three registers in the 6510 to make the screen flash, swapping the border and screen colours. To stop the program, press Run/Stop and Restore.

```
.A 3000 LDA $D021  : Load 'A' with the value in $D021
.A 3003 TAX        : Transfer it to 'X'
.A 3004 LDA $D020  : Load 'A' with the value in $D020
.A 3007 TAY        : Transfer it to 'Y'
.A 3008 STX $D020  : Store the value in 'X' in $D020
.A 300B STY $D021  : Store the value in 'Y' in $D021
.A 300E JMP $3000  : Jump to address $3000
```

The above program is a simple example of how numbers may be swapped with another in machine code.

We will often find during a program that we want to add one to something. Well, the 6510 makes it easy for us. It increments (adds one to) registers or memory locations. Here are the commands you'll need to use:

INC $ memory location : Adds one to the value contained in the memory location. If the number exceeds 255, which is the greatest number that a memory location (or register) can hold, then the number has 256 subtracted from it.

INX : Adds one to the contents of the 'X' register. If the value exceeds 255, then 256 is subtracted from it.

INY : Adds one to the contents of the 'Y' register. If the value exceeds 255, then 256 is subtracted from it.

26

We can also automatically subtract one from the memory location or the register. If the number becomes less than zero, then 256 is added to it. The relevant commands are as follows.

DEC $ memory location : Subtracts one from 'memory location'.
DEX   : Subtracts one from the 'X' register.
DEY   : Subtracts one from the 'Y' register.

Here is a program that cycles the screen and border through all 256 colour combinations.

```
.A 2F00 INC $D020   : Increment value in $D020
.A 2F03 DEC $D021   : Decrement value in $D021
.A 2F06 JMP $2F00   : Jump to $2F00
```

To stop the above program, press Run/Stop and Restore and re-enter the assembler with 'SYS 38893'.

Say you only want to increment the number by a certain amount, you need a method of checking when you get to that number. There are commands in the 6510 which allow you to compare two values. They are as follows:

CMP #$ value : Compare memory or Accumulator with a value.

CMP $ memory location : Compare the value in 'memory location' with the value in the Accumulator.

CPX #$ value : Compare memory or the 'X' register with a value.

CPX $ memory location : Compare the value in 'memory location' with the value in the 'X' register.

CPY #$ value : Compare memory or Accumulator with the value in the 'Y' register.

CPY $ memory location : Compare the value in 'memory location' with the value in the 'Y' register.

27

The above commands set various flags in the status register. The status register contains eight flags but at the moment we are concerned with only three of them. They are the overflow flag, the sign flag and the zero flag.

The zero flag is set if the Accumulator is zero or if the value in a register is the same as that which is being compared using the 'CMP', 'CPX' or 'CPY' commands.

The overflow flag is set when an overflow happens, ie. when a calculation passes 255 ($FF) or zero ($00).

The sign flag is set according to whether a number in one of the registers is greater than or less than 128 ($80). If the number is greater than or equal to 128 then the flag is set; otherwise it is zero.

Now, once we have done a comparison we may want to do something according to the result. There are commands within the 6510 to do this. They are as follows:

BEQ $ memory location : Branch (jump) to 'memory location' if the last byte used in X, Y, A or a memory location is zero or zero flag is set (i.e. values are equal). This command only allows jumps of 128 forward and 127 back. If the address after the 'BEQ' command is greater than 128 forward then the branch will be backward.

BNE $ memory location : Branch to memory location if the last byte in X, Y, A or a memory location is not equal to zero, does not contain zero or a comparison is not equal. The limitation of 128 forward and 127 back also applies to this command.

BCC $ memory location : Branch to 'memory location' if the last byte in X, Y, A or a memory location is less than or equal to that compared with, or the carry flag is clear.

28

BCS $ memory location : Branch to 'memory location' if the last byte in X, Y, A or a memory location is greater than or equal to that compared, or the carry flag is set.

BVS $ memory location : Branch if the overflow flag is set. The same limitation for branching applies.

BVC $ memory location : Branch if the overflow flag is not set. The same limitation for branching applies.

BPL $ memory location : Branch if the value in a register is greater than 128. The same limitation for branching applies.

BMI $ memory location : Branch if the value in a register is less than 128. The same limitation for branching applies.

Here follows a program that demonstrates the use of some of the above commands in use.

```
.A 1000 LDX #$00     : Load 'X' with 00 Hex
.A 1002 STX $D020    : Store value in 'X' in $D020
.A 1005 INX          : Increment value in 'X'
.A 1006 CPX #$0F     : Is value in 'X' #$0F (255)
.A 1008 BNE $1002    : No? Then jump to $1002
.A 100A LDY #$0F     : Load 'Y' with #$0F
.A 100C STY $D021    : Store value in 'Y' in $D021
.A 100F DEY          : Decrement value in 'Y'
.A 1010 CPY #$01     : Is value in 'Y' #$01 (1)
.A 1012 BNE $100C    : No? Then jump to $100C
.A 1014 LDA $C5      : Load 'A' with value in $C5
.A 1016 CMP #$04     : Is value in 'A' #$04 (4)
.A 1018 BNE $1000    : No? Start all over again
.A 101A RTS          : Return to BASIC.
```

The above program flashes the screen and border colours, and if the 'F1' function key is being pressed returns to BASIC. If it is not then the program starts all over again.

When you are testing a program using the assembler, you will often want to return control to the assembler automatically. This can be done quite easily in a program by inserting the command 'BRK' into it. If the assembler has not been enabled then the result of this command will be that the computer will do the equivalent of pressing Run/Stop and Restore.

The 6510 has a part of memory that is specially used for storing numbers. It is called the 'stack'. It is 256 bytes long and is located from 256 (dec) to 511 (dec). It is a first-in-last-out area, i.e. the first number put on the stack is the last to come out and *vice versa*. There are six commands that you can use for the stack, and they are as follows:

PHA : Puts the contents of the Accumulator on to the top of the stack.

PLA : Takes the number off the top of the stack and puts it into the Accumulator.

PHP : Puts the processor status (the flags that are set) on to the top of the stack.

PLP : Takes the processor status off the top of the stack and puts it into the status flag.

TXS : Sets the stack pointer to the location 256 plus the value in 'X'. This is useful if you want to ignore certain elements on the stack or if you want to pick selected elements off the stack.

TSX : Puts the value of the stack pointer into the 'X' register.

Here is a program that demonstrates the use of the stack:

.A 6000 LDA #$93   : Load 'A' with #$93 (147)
.A 6002 PHA   : Put on to the stack
.A 6003 LDA #$41   : Load 'A' with #$41 (65)
.A 6005 LDX #$00   : Load 'X' with #$00 (0)
.A 6007 JSR $FFD2 : Jump to the PRINT subroutine
.A 600A INX   : Increment the value in 'X'
.A 600B BNE $6007 : is 'X'=0. No? Jump to $6007
.A 600D LDA $C5   : Load 'A' with value in $C5
.A 600F CMP #$40   : Is it $40 (64)

30

```
.A 6011 BNE $600D : No? Jump to $600D
.A 6013 PLA        : Get top number off the stack
.A 6014 JSR $FFD2 : Jump to the PRINT subroutine
.A 6017 RTS        : Return to BASIC
```

The above program prints 256 'a' characters on the screen and pauses for a key to be pressed. It then takes the top value off the stack and prints it (i.e. clears the screen).

Now it is time to delve into the various addressing modes. We have already covered three of them:

1. **Immediate addressing:** This is where the value after the operand (6510 command) is a constant.

```
eg. LDA #$00
    LDX #$FF
    CMP #$0F
```

2. **Absolute addressing:** This is where the value after the operand is an address.

```
eg. LDA $033C
    STA $D022
    CMP $D000
```

3. **Zero Page addressing:** This is where the value after the operand is an address in zero page ($00–$FF (0–255)).

```
eg. LDA $C5
    STA $FB
    CMP $C5
```

The fourth addressing mode is called Indexed addressing. This is where the operand is an address, but it can be altered depending on the value in one of the index registers (i.e. 'X' or 'Y').

```
eg. LDA $0400,X
```

If the 'X' register contained $12 then the Accumulator would be loaded with the value in address $0400+$12 (which is $0412). If this seems strange then think of it as LDA '$0400+value in 'X".

31

Here is a small program that fills the top 200 bytes of the screen with circular shapes:

```
.A 1000 LDX #$00        : Load 'X' with $00 (00 dec)
.A 1002 LDA #$51        : Load 'A' with $51 (81 dec)
.A 1004 STA $0400,X     : Store it in $0400+X
.A 1007 LDA #$01        : Load 'A' with $01 (1 dec)
.A 1009 STA $D800,X     : Store it in $d800+X
.A 100C INX             : Increment value in 'X'
.A 100D CPX #$C8        : Is 'X' #$C8 (200 dec)
.A 100F BNE $1002       : No? Jump to $1002
.A 1011 RTS             : Return to BASIC
```

Here is a list of the commands covered earlier using the Indexed addressing mode:

LDA $04,X   : Load 'A' with the value in $04+X.
LDA $0400,X   : Load 'A' with the value in $0400+X.
LDA $0400,Y   : Load 'A' with the value in $0400+Y.

STA $CC,X   : Store the value in 'A' in $CC+X.
STA $D800,X   : Store the value in 'A' in $D800+X.
STA $D000,Y   : Store the value in 'A' in $D000+Y.

LDX $D0,Y   : Load 'X' with the value in $D0+Y.
LDX $2000,Y   : Load 'X' with the value in $2000+Y.

STX $BB,Y   : Store the value in 'X' in $BB+Y.

LDY $AA,X   : Load 'Y' with the value in $AA+X.
LDY $DFAA,X   : Load 'Y' with the value in $DFAA+X.

STY $EE,X   : Store the value in 'X' in $EE+X.

INC $00,X   : Increment the value in $00+X.
INC $F000,X   : Increment the value in $F000+X.

DEC $AD,X   : Decrement the value in $AD+X.
DEC $D001,X   : Decrement the value in $D001+X.

```
CMP $00,X      : Compare the value in $00 with 'A'.
CMP $D020,X    : Compare the value in $D020+X with 'A'.
CMP $AA00,Y    : Compare the value in $AA00+Y with 'A'.
```

There are two more addressing modes in the 6510; they are also the most complex. They are Indexed Indirect addressing and Indirect Indexed addressing.

The Indexed Indirect addressing mode does not follow the normal formats of addressing—it does it through two other locations in the zero page (hence the indirect part of its name). However, it can only use the 'A' and 'X' registers. Here is an example:

```
LDX #$00       : Normal LDX.
LDA ($FB,X)    : Indexed Indirect LDA.
```

The above 'LDA' would load the Accumulator from the address in 6510 low/high byte in $FB+X.

Let me explain. The address which will be loaded from is not $FB but it *is* contained in $FB AND $FC. For example, suppose that $FB contained zero, $FC contained $04 and X contained zero, 'A' would be loaded from the addresses contained in $FB and $FC, i.e. 0400 (low byte=00 and high byte=$04). This would therefore be equivalent to LDA $0400. The value in 'X' is added to the $FB so that 'X' contained $02, then 'A' would be loaded from the address contained in $FB+$02 and $FC+$02, which is $FD and $FE.

Why then use this mode if it appears the same as LDA $0400. Well, this mode allows us to access all 64K of memory in one command.

Here is a program that fills the entire screen with '@' characters in one loop:

```
.A 2500 LDA #$00    : Load 'A' with #$00
.A 2502 STA $FB     : Store 'A' in $FB
.A 2504 STA $FD     : Store 'A' in $FD
```

```
.A 2506 LDA #$04        : Load 'A' with #$04
.A 2508 STA $FC         : Store 'A' in $FC
.A 250A LDA #$D8        : Load 'A' with $D8
.A 250C STA $FE         : Store 'A' in $FE
.A 250E LDX #$00        : Load 'X' with #$00
.A 2510 LDA #$00        : Load 'A' with #$00
.A 2512 STA ($FB,X)     : Store 'A' through $FB, $FC
.A 2514 LDA #$01        : Load 'A' with #$01
.A 2516 STA ($FD,X)     : Store 'A' through $FD, $FE
.A 2518 INC $FB         : Increment the value in $FB
.A 251A INC $FD         : Increment the value in $FD
.A 251C LDA $FB         : Load 'A' with the value in $FB
.A 251E BNE $2510       : Is 'A' zero? No? Jump to $2510
.A 2520 INC $FC         : Increment the value in $FC
.A 2522 INC $FE         : Increment the value in $FE
.A 2524 LDA $FC         : Load 'A' with the value in $FC
.A 2526 CMP #$08        : Is it #$08?
.A 2528 BNE $2510       : No? Then branch to $2510
.A 252A RTS             : Return to BASIC
```

The first six commands are necessary to set up the locations $FB to $FE to the values required by the program.

Here is a list of all the commands covered so far in Indexed Indirect mode:

LDA ($01,X)   : Load 'A' with the value from the address contained in $01+X and $02+X.

STA ($DA,X)   : Store the value in 'A' in the address contained in $DA+X and $DB+X.

CMP ($F1,X)   : Compare the value in 'A' with the value in the address contained in $F1+X and $F2+X.

Now before we come to the final addressing mode there is an addressing mode which really does not merit its own section as it affects only one command. It is an Indirect mode, i.e. the actual address to be used is contained in two other addresses anywhere in memory. Unlike other indirect modes it can jump through any memory address ($0000 to

$FFFF), e.g. JMP ($0314). It is mainly used where a program can jump to one of many addresses depending upon the result of a calculation or input from the user. Here follows an example which demonstrates the use of the above command:

```
.A 2100 LDA $C5       : Load 'A' with the value in $C5
.A 2102 CMP #$3C      : Is it #$3C (60)?
.A 2104 BNE $2113     : No? Then jump to $2213
.A 2106 LDA #$31      : Load 'A' with #$31 (48)
.A 2108 STA $033C     : Store the value in 'A' in $033C
.A 210B LDA #$21      : Load 'A' with #$21 (33)
.A 210D STA $033D     : Store the value in 'A' in $033D
.A 2110 JMP $212B     : Jump to $212B
.A 2113 CMP #$04      : Is it #$04 (4)?
.A 2115 BNE $2124     : No? Then jump to $2220
.A 2117 LDA #$39      : Load 'A' with #$40(64)
.A 2119 STA $033C     : Store the value in 'A' in $033C
.A 211C LDA #$21      : Load 'A' with #$21(33)
.A 211E STA $033D     : Store the value in 'A' in $033D
.A 2121 JMP $212B     : Jump to $212B
.A 2124 CMP #$01(?)   : Is it #$01 (1)
.A 2126 BNE $212E     : No? Jump to $212E
.A 2128 JMP $2141     : Jump to $2100
.A 212B JMP ($033C)   : Jump   through   $033C   and
                        $033D
.A 212E JMP $2100     : Jump to $2100 (start again)
.A 2131 LDA #$02      : Load 'A' with #$02 (2)
.A 2133 STA $D020     : Store the value in 'A' in $D020
.A 2136 JMP $212E     : Jump to $212E
.A 2139 LDA #$00      : Load 'A' with #$00
.A 213B STA $D020     : Store the value in 'A' in $D020
.A 213E JMP $212E     : Jump to $212E
.A 2141 RTS           : Return to BASIC
```

The above program alters the border colour according to which key is pressed: if the key pressed is the Space Bar then the screen will turn red; if the key is 'F1' then the screen will turn black; and finally, if the key is the return key, then control will be passed back to BASIC.

Let us now move onto the final mode of addressing on the 6510 chip. It is called Indirect Indexed addressing and only makes use of the Accumulator and the 'Y' register. This mode of addressing is very similar to Indexed Indirect except for two things, the first of which is that the 'Y' register is used instead of the 'X'. And secondly, it is the actual address that has the value in the 'Y' register added to it, not the zero page addresses through which the actual address is found. The actual address is stored in the same low/high byte order within zero page.

Here is an example:

LDA ($CA),Y

If $CA contained #$10, $CB contained $C0 and 'Y' contained $10, then the actual address would be equal to $C010 added to $10, which is $C010.

Here is a program that changes all the characters on the screen to each of the 16 colours using Indirect Indexed addressing:

```
3000 A9 00      LDA #$00  : Load 'A' with #$00 (0)
3002 8D 3E 03   STA $033E : Store 'A' in $033E (830)
3005 A9 00      LDA #$00  : Load 'A' with #$00 (0)
3007 85 FB      STA $FB   : Store 'A' in $FB (251)
3009 A9 D8      LDA #$D8  : Load 'A' with #$D8
                            (216)
300B 85 FC      STA $FC   : Store 'A' in $FC (252)
300D A9 E7      LDA #$E7  : Load 'A' with #$E7
                            (231)
300F 8D 3C 03   STA $033C : Store 'A' in $033C (828)
3012 A9 DB      LDA #$DB  : Load 'A' with #$DB
                            (219)
3014 8D 3D 03   STA $033D : Store 'A' in $033D (829)
3017 A0 00      LDY #$00  : Load 'Y' with #$00 (0)
3019 AD 3E 03   LDA $033E : Load 'A' with the value
                            in $033E
301C 91 FB      STA
                ($FB),Y   : Store 'A' indirectly in
                            $FB,$FC
```

```
301E 20 35 30   JSR $3035 : Jump to the subroutine
                            at $3035
3021 A5 FB      LDA $FB   : Load 'A' with the value
                            in $FB
3023 CD 3C 03   CMP $033C : Is 'A' equal to the value
                            in $033C
3026 F0 03      BEQ $302B : Yes? Branch to $302B
3028 4C 17 30   JMP $3017 : Jump to $3017
302B A5 FC      LDA $FC   : Load 'A' with the value
                            in $FC
302D CD 3D 03   CMP $033D : Is 'A' equal to the value
                            in $033D
3030 F0 0B      BEQ $303D : Yes? Branch to $303D
3032 4C 17 30   JMP $3017 : Jump to $3017
3035 E6 FB      INC $FB   : Increment the value in
                            $FB
3037 F0 01      BEQ $303A : Is $FB equal to zero?
                            Then branch to $303A
3039 60         RTS       : Return from subroutine
303A E6 FC      INC $FC   : Increment the value in
                            $FC
303C 60         RTS       : Return from subroutine
303D EE 3E 03   INC $033E : Increment the value in
                            $033E
3040 AD 3E 03   LDA $033E : Load 'A' with the value
                            in $033E
3043 C9 11      CMP #$11  : Is it #$11
3045 F0 09      BEQ $3050 : Yes? Branch to $3050
3047 A5 C5      LDA $C5   : Load 'A' with the value
                            in $C5
3049 C9 40      CMP #$40  : Is it #$40
304B F0 FA      BEQ $3047 : Yes? Branch to $3047
304D 4C 05 30   JMP $3005 : Jump to $3005
3050 60         RTS       : Return to BASIC
```

The above program will fill the screen with one colour and wait for you to press a key. It will then fill the screen with the next colour and wait again for a keypress . . . and so on, until $0286 contains $0F (15). It will then return to BASIC.

Here is a list of all the commands covered so far in Indirect Indexed mode:

LDA ($D0),Y : Load 'A' with the value in the address contained in addresses $D0 and $D1.

STA ($FE),Y : Store the value in 'A' in the address contained in addresses $FE and $FF.

CMP ($02),Y : Compare the value in 'A' with the value in the address contained in $02 and $03.

Now we come to the logical operators. These are the commands that allow us to programme using the bits of a program, and not just the bytes; this is done when using sprites (even in BASIC) for example. All logical commands work with the Accumulator only.

Firstly the command 'AND', which is identical to its equivalent in BASIC. It takes two binary numbers and if the bit is one in both numbers, then the result is a one, else it is a zero.

eg.	Binary	Decimal
	10111011	187
AND	11000101	197
	10000001	129

As you can see 'AND' can be used for sectioning parts of bytes off from the others (for example, if you want to check if sprite '1' is on but don't really care if the rest are or not).

Next the command 'ORA', which is the same as the BASIC keyword 'OR'. It takes two binary numbers and if the bit is one in either number, then the result is one.

eg.	Binary	Decimal
	11010011	211
ORA	10100010	162
	11110011	243

This command is usually used to set certain bits without affecting the others in the byte (for example to turn on sprite '3' and leave the others as they are).

Now we will cover the command 'EOR' (Exclusive OR). This command has no equivalent BASIC keyword but is nevertheless just as simple to understand as it performs the opposite function to 'ORA' command. It takes two binary numbers and if one of the numbers is a '1' then the result is a '1'. However, if neither or both are one then the result is a zero.

This command could be used in the high resolution plotting of a shape, so that the shape could pass over the background without disturbing it.

Finally on the subject of logical commands we move on to 'BIT'. This command performs the same function as 'AND' but only alters the status flags, leaving the two bytes being 'ANDed' the same as they were.

Here is a list of all the above commands in all the different addressing modes:

AND #$01   : AND the value in 'A' with #$01.
AND $DD,X   : AND the value in 'A' with the value in $DD+X.
AND $C020   : AND the value in 'A' with the value in $C020.
AND $D000,X   : AND the value in 'A' with the value in $D000+X.
AND $F000,Y   : AND the value in 'A' with the value in $F000+Y.
AND ($AA,X)   : AND the value in 'A' with the value in the address in $AA+X and $AB+X.
AND ($11),Y   : AND the value in 'A' with the value in the 'address+Y' in $11 and $12.
ORA #$F0   : OR the value in 'A' with #$F0.
ORA $00   : OR the value in 'A' with the value in $00.
ORA $B2,X   : OR the value in 'A' with the value in $B2+X.

ORA $8010	: OR the value in 'A' with the value in $8010.
ORA $2011,X	: OR the value in 'A' with the value in $2011+X.
ORA $DDDD,Y	: OR the value in 'A' with the value in $DDDD+Y.
ORA ($BB,X)	: OR the value in 'A' with the value in the address contained in $BB+X and $BC+X.
ORA ($33),Y	: OR the value in 'A' with the value in the 'address+Y' contained in $33 and $34.
EOR #$00	: EOR the value in 'A' with #$00.
EOR $D1	: EOR the value in 'A' with the value in $01.
EOR $EE,X	: EOR the value in 'A' with the value in $EE+X.
EOR $0000	: EOR the value in 'A' with the value in $0000.
EOR $1020,X	: EOR the value in 'A' with the value in $1020+X.
EOR $A000,Y	: EOR the value in 'A' with the value in $A000+Y.
EOR ($CC,X)	: EOR the value in 'A' with the value in the address contained in $CC+X and $CD+X.
EOR ($22),Y	: EOR the value in 'A' with the value in the 'address+Y' contained in $22 and $23.
BIT $AE	: AND the value in 'A' with the value in $AE and adjust the flags leaving the contents of 'A' and $AE intact.
BIT $DA0E	: AND the value in 'A' with the value in $DA0E and adjust the flags leaving the contents of 'A' and $DA0E intact.

Now we come to the arithmetic commands. These allow adding and subtracting in machine code. Firstly, let's consider addition.

On the 6510, a register can only hold a value of between zero and 255—so the following commands can only come up with a result of between zero and 255. Later we will find a way of getting around this problem.

The command for addition is 'ADC'. This means ADd with

Carry. This carry is a flag in the status register that tells us if the result is greater than 255. For example, if we added 129 and 128 the result would be '2' in the Accumulator but the carry flag would be set. The carry therefore acts as a ninth bit. It tells us that the result is '256+1' which is 257. We can then add numbers up to 511 (256+255).

Here is an example of adding two numbers together and POKEing the character associated with that number at the top of the screen:

```
.A 1000 LDA #$01    : Load 'A' with #$01 (1)
.A 1002 CLC         : Clear the carry flag
.A 1003 ADC #$02    : Add #$02 to the value in 'A'
.A 1005 STA $0400   : Store the value in 'A' in $0400
.A 1008 LDA #$01    : Load 'A' with #$01 (1)
.A 100A STA D800    : Store 'A' in $D800 (55296)
.A 100B RTS         : Return to BASIC
```

The 'CLC' command in the above program may cause confusion. What it does is clear the carry flag. This is needed in the above example as we are only adding two numbers. If, however, there was an ADC before our program we might have wanted the carry (bit nine—value 256) to be added to our result if the value was greater than 255. So we must use the 'CLC' command when we want to ignore what is in the carry flag or before the first addition.

Now we come to subtraction. This command works in basically the same way as 'ADC' in that if the carry flag is set and you subtract, the carry is set if the number goes below zero. The command is 'SBC'. . .SuBtract with Carry. However, unlike addition we have to set the carry flag in order to make a correct subtraction. This is done with the 'SEC' (SEt Carry) command.

Here is a program that demonstrates the 'SBC' command in use. It subtracts two numbers and POKEs the character associated with the result at the top of the screen:

```
.A 1200 LDA #$20    : Load 'A' with #$20 (32)
.A 1202 SEC         : Set the carry flag
.A 1203 SBC #$18    : Subtract #$18 from the value in
                      'A'
```

```
.A 1205 STA $0400      : Store the value in $0400 (1024)
.A 1208 LDA #$01       : Load 'A' with #$01 (1)
.A 120A STA $D800      : Store the value in 'A' in $D800
.A 120B RTS            : Return to BASIC
```

Here is a list of the two commands in all the addressing modes of the 6510 (C refers to the carry flag):

ADC #$01   : Add #$01 to the value in 'A' with carry and put the result in 'A'.

ADC $21   : Add the value in $21 to the value in 'A' with carry and put the result in 'A'.

ADC $78,Y   : Add the value in '$78+Y' to the value in 'A' with carry and put the result in 'A'.

ADC $CBA1   : Add the value in $CBA1 to the value in 'A' with carry and put the result in 'A'.

ADC $2011,X   : Add the value in '$2011+X' to the value in 'A' with carry and put the result in 'A'.

ADC $323A,Y   : Add the value in '$323A+Y' to the value in 'A' with carry and put the result in 'A'.

ADC ($56,X)   : Add the value in the address contained in '$56+X' and '$57+X' with carry and put the result in 'A'.

ADC ($FA),Y   : Add the value in the 'address+Y' contained in $FA and $FB with carry and put the result in 'A'.

SBC #$8F   : Subtract the value in #$18 from the value in 'A' with carry and put the result in 'A'.

SBC $DC   : Subtract the value in $DC from the value in 'A' with carry and put the result in 'A'.

SBC $0785   : Subtract the value in $0785 from the value in 'A' with carry and put the result in 'A'.

SBC $FF02,X   : Subtract the value in '$FF02+X' from the value in 'A' with carry and put the result in 'A'.

SBC $A023,Y   : Subtract the value in '$A023+Y' from the value in 'A' with carry and put the result in 'A'.

SBC ($AA,X)   : Subtract the value in the address contained in '$AA+X' and '$AB+X' from the value in 'A' with carry and put the result in 'A'.

SBC ($B0),Y : Subtract the value in the 'address+Y' contained in $B0 and $B1 from the value in 'A' with carry and put the result in 'A'.

In the 6510 all of the flags can be turned on or off by the user. We have seen the use of 'CLC' and 'SEC' to clear the carry flag and set it respectively. Here is a list of the other commands for setting or clearing flags:

SED : Set the decimal mode flag. (See BCD arithmetic.)
CLD : Clear the decimal mode flag.
SEI : Set the interrupt disable flag. (See Interrupts.)
CLI : Clear the interrupt disable flag.
CLV : Clear the overflow flag.

Before we continue there is one command that I need to cover but it does not fit into the above listing. It is 'RTI'. This command means ReTurn from Interrupt. This command causes control to return to the program being RUN from an 'IRQ' interrupt. (See Interrupts.)

Now we come to the commands that allow us to manipulate the bits inside a register or a memory location. The first is 'ROR'. This command means ROtate the bits to the Right. It follows the pattern shown in the following diagram:

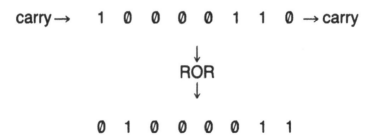

```
carry→   1  0  0  0  0  1  1  0  → carry
                      ↓
                     ROR
                      ↓
         0  1  0  0  0  0  1  1
```

There is a complementary command to 'ROR' and it is called 'ROL'. This command means ROtate the bits to the Left, and it follows the pattern shown in the following diagram:

43

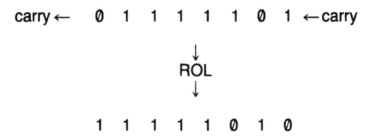

```
carry ←   0  1  1  1  1  1  0  1  ←carry

                    ↓
                  ROL
                    ↓

          1  1  1  1  1  0  1  0
```

There are another two commands that do the same as the above but do not bring the bits around. Therefore, they are useful for sectioning off half-bytes for examining. (See BCD arithmetic.) The first of these is 'ASL', which means Arithmetic Shift Left. The following diagram shows what happens with 'ASL':

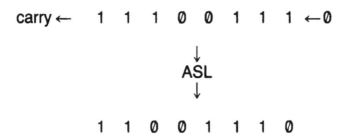

```
carry ←   1  1  1  0  0  1  1  1  ←0

                    ↓
                  ASL
                    ↓

          1  1  0  0  1  1  1  0
```

There is a complementary command to 'ASL' called 'LSR', which means Logical Shift Right. It follows the pattern shown in the following diagram:

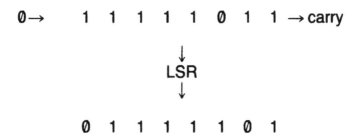

```
0→        1  1  1  1  1  0  1  1  → carry

                    ↓
                  LSR
                    ↓

          0  1  1  1  1  1  0  1
```

Now we have covered all the 6510 instruction set, let us go and do something useful with the knowledge we have gained. . .

SECTION TWO

This section will make use of all the knowledge gained in Section 1 allowing the '64 do great things in machine code. All of the programs in this section should be entered with an assembler/monitor such as *SUPERMON*.

SCROLLING

Often in games we will want to scroll the screen, eg. see *Defender, Scramble, The Riders of Rohan,* and similar games. This really needs to be done in machine code for reasons of speed. The following programs will scroll the screen up, down, left and right, by both a character and a pixel at a time.

To scroll the screen up one character square, all we are really doing is executing the BASIC command PRINT. However, in machine code we need to tell the computer what to print. In this case we need to make the computer print a carriage return (move the contents of the screen up one position). But this will only work if the cursor is positioned on the bottom line of the screen—thus we print 24 carriage return characters before starting to scroll:

```
2000 A2 00        LDX #$00
2002 A9 0D        LDA #$0D
2004 20 D2 FF     JSR $FFD2
2007 E8           INX
2008 E0 12        CPX #$12
200A D0 F8        BNE $2004
200C 60           RTS
  .
  .
  .
```

Before starting the scroll SYS 8192 ($2000) to set the screen up.

Now, the scroll routine:

```
  .
200D A9 0D        LDA #$0D
200F 20 D2 FF     JSR $FFD2
2012 60           RTS
  .
  .
```

46

To save the above to tape, type:

S"DOWNSCROLL",01,2000,2013

and to disk:

S"DOWNSCROLL",08,2000,2013

The reason that the last Hex number is one greater than the last byte of program is that the save routine in the ROM that the monitor calls saves up to but not including the last number—therefore, it will save from $2000 to $2012.

To scroll the contents of the screen up, just type SYS 8205 (JSR $200D). The new data to be put on the screen must now be put on the bottom line of the screen.

The following program scrolls the contents of the screen down one character space, but does not scroll the top two lines. The reason for this is that location 218 is set, so that we can put information that we do not want scrolled on these two lines and scroll the rest of the screen. Basically, a window is created in which the top two lines are separated from the rest of the screen.

```
4000 A9 13       LDA #$13
4002 20 D2 FF    JSR $FFD2
4005 A9 11       LDA #$11
4007 20 D2 FF    JSR $FFD2
400A A9 9D       LDA #$9D
400C 20 D2 FF    JSR $FFD2
400F A9 94       LDA #$94
4011 20 D2 FF    JSR $FFD2
4014 A9 80       LDA #$80
4016 85 DA       STA $DA
4018 60          RTS
 .
```

The above program is the same as the following in BASIC, so any program in BASIC that contains the following lines could be replaced by the above program to give it that extra lift.

```
10 PRINT "[home][cud][left][inst]"
20 POKE218,128
```

No setting up is needed for this program, unlike the scroll-up.

Now we come to the scrolling operation that proves most popular in many programs. . . scrolling sideways. This is more complex than the above as there is no way of using the 'PRINT' command to achieve sideways scrolling with enough speed to be useful. It can be done in BASIC as long as you do not want to scroll the bottom line of the screen, but it takes so long that writing a word processing program or a game would be pointless without machine code.

The following program scrolls the screen to the right. It is written in a very simple manner to show exactly what is going on. All the program does is take a character from a screen location and put it into the one on its right.

```
·
1000 A2 26          LDX #$26
1002 BD 00 04       LDA $0400,X
1005 9D 01 04       STA $0401,X
1008 BD 28 04       LDA $0428,X
100B 9D 29 04       STA $0429,X
100E BD 50 04       LDA $0450,X
1011 9D 51 04       STA $0451,X
1014 BD 78 04       LDA $0478,X
1017 9D 79 04       STA $0479,X
101A BD A0 04       LDA $04A0,X
101D 9D A1 04       STA $04A1,X
1020 BD C8 04       LDA $04C8,X
1023 9D C9 04       STA $04C9,X
1026 BD F0 04       LDA $04F0,X
1029 9D F1 04       STA $04F1,X
102C BD 18 05       LDA $0518,X
102F 9D 19 05       STA $0519,X
1032 BD 40 05       LDA $0540,X
1035 9D 41 05       STA $0541,X
```

48

```
1038 BD 68 05        LDA $0568,X
103B 9D 69 05        STA $0569,X
103E BD 90 05        LDA $0590,X
1041 9D 91 05        STA $0591,X
1044 BD B8 05        LDA $05B8,X
1047 9D B9 05        STA $05B9,X
104A BD E0 05        LDA $05E0,X
104D 9D E1 05        STA $05E1,X
1050 BD 08 06        LDA $0608,X
1053 9D 09 06        STA $0609,X
1056 BD 30 06        LDA $0630,X
1059 9D 31 06        STA $0631,X
105C BD 58 06        LDA $0658,X
105F 9D 59 06        STA $0659,X
1062 BD 80 06        LDA $0680,X
1065 9D 81 06        STA $0681,X
1068 BD A8 06        LDA $06A8,X
106B 9D A9 06        STA $06A9,X
106E BD D0 06        LDA $06D0,X
1071 9D D1 06        STA $06D1,X
1074 BD F8 06        LDA $06F8,X
1077 9D F9 06        STA $06F9,X
107A BD 20 07        LDA $0720,X
107D 9D 21 07        STA $0721,X
1080 BD 48 07        LDA $0748,X
1083 9D 49 07        STA $0749,X
1086 BD 70 07        LDA $0770,X
1089 9D 71 07        STA $0771,X
108C BD 98 07        LDA $0798,X
108F 9D 99 07        STA $0799,X
1092 BD C0 07        LDA $07C0,X
1095 9D C1 07        STA $07C1,X
1098 CA             DEX
1099 E0 FF          CPX #$FF
109B F0 03          BEQ $10A0
109D 4C 02 10       JMP $1002
10A0 60             RTS
```

As you can see, the above program is long-winded and takes up far more memory than is needed. Instead of lots of 'LDA' and 'STA' commands, we really only need four of each. What we want to do is scroll each line by a character space but we don't want the end character on a line to be moved onto the next line down. To achieve this we just add one to the X register and carry on until the next line is completed. When the next line is finished, we repeat the above until the end of the screen, then we RTS to BASIC (or Machine Code program, depending on where the routine was called from).

The following program uses the above method to scroll the whole of the screen to the left. You will notice that the program is much smaller yet does the same job. Unluckily, you may not find the way that it works as obvious when looking at the listing as with the previous program, but it is slightly faster and definitely neater.

```
        .
        .
1000  A9  06        LDA  #$06
1002  8D  44  03    STA  $0344
1005  A2  00        LDX  #$00
1007  A0  00        LDY  #$00
1009  BD  01  04    LDA  $0401,X
100C  9D  00  04    STA  $0400,X
100F  BD  F1  04    LDA  $04F1,X
1012  9D  F0  04    STA  $04F0,X
1015  BD  E1  05    LDA  $05E1,X
1018  9D  E0  05    STA  $05E0,X
101B  BD  D1  06    LDA  $06D1,X
101E  9D  D0  06    STA  $06D0,X
1021  E8           INX
1022  C8           INY
1023  C0  27        CPY  #$27
1025  D0  E2        BNE  $1009
1027  E8           INX
1028  A0  00        LDY  #$00
102A  CE  44  03    DEC  $0344
102D  D0  DA        BNE  $1009
102F  60           RTS
```

PIXEL SCROLLING

Pixel scrolling does the same job as the scrolling programs just mentioned, except that it moves the characters by one pixel (or dot) at a time—therefore, giving a much smoother, professional look to programs.

We will start with up and down scrolling as before. Pixel scrolling on the Commodore 64 is handled mainly by hardware (the VIC 2 chip) but does need a helping hand to complete the scroll. By this I mean the chip will move the entire contents of the screen by up to seven pixels. When it reaches the eighth it cannot go any further and so goes back to zero. We therefore have to set it back to position zero and do a character scroll to move the screen the last bit. For up and down scrolling the register we are interested in is 53265

Now if we just scrolled the screen without any set-up you would notice that there would be spaces at the top and bottom of the screen. Ideally, the display should look perfect, so we want to get rid of these spaces. This is done by setting the '64 into 24-row mode. This cuts off the top half character space from the screen and the bottom half character space. This now allows the characters to come onto the screen and leave smoothly without any gaps.

To put the '64 into 24-row mode, type the following:

```
A 3000 LDA $D011

A 3003 AND #$F7

A 3005 STA $D011

A 3008 RTS
```

51

To get back into 25-row mode, type the following:

```
A 3000 LDA $D011

A 3003 ORA #$08

A 3005 STA 53265

A 3008 RTS
```

The following program is a pixel scroll routine in the up direction. It works by decrementing the value in a location (which is where the position of the scroll is kept) and when this value reaches #$FF it resets the counter location to seven and performs a character scroll to move the screen the final pixel.

```
.
.
4000 AD 11 D0      LDA $D011
4003 29 F7         AND #$F7
4005 8D 11 D0      STA $D011
4008 A9 07         LDA #$07
400A 8D 3B 40      STA $403B
400D 60            RTS
400E AD 11 D0      LDA $D011
4011 29 F8         AND #$F8
4013 18            CLC
4014 6D 3B 40      ADC $403B
4017 8D 11 D0      STA $D011
401A CE 3B 40      DEC $403B
401D AD 3B 40      LDA $403B
4020 C9 FF         CMP #$FF
4022 F0 01         BEQ $4025
4024 60            RTS
4025 A9 07         LDA #$07
4027 8D 3B 40      STA $403B
402A AD 11 D0      LDA $D011
402D 29 F8         AND #$F8
402F 18            CLC
4030 69 07         ADC #$07
```

```
4032 8D 11 D0        STA $D011
4035 A9 0D           LDA #$0D
4037 20 D2 FF        JSR $FFD2
403A 60              RTS
403B 07              ???
```

Now for the pixel scroll downwards. It works in exactly the same way as the up scroll, except that it increments the counter until it reaches eight and then resets the counter to zero and performs the character scroll down.

```
.
4000 AD 11 D0        LDA $D011
4003 29 F7           AND #$F7
4005 8D 11 D0        STA $D011
4008 A9 00           LDA #$00
400A 8D 4B 40        STA $404B
400D 60              RTS
400E AD 11 D0        LDA $D011
4011 29 F8           AND #$F8
4013 18              CLC
4014 6D 4B 40        ADC $404B
4017 8D 11 D0        STA $D011
401A EE 4B 40        INC $404B
401D AD 4B 40        LDA $404B
4020 C9 08           CMP #$08
4022 F0 01           BEQ $4025
4024 60              RTS
4025 A9 00           LDA #$00
4027 8D 4B 40        STA $404B
402A AD 11 D0        LDA $D011
402D 29 F8           AND #$F8
402F 8D 11 D0        STA $D011
4032 A9 13           LDA #$13
4034 20 D2 FF        JSR $FFD2
4037 A9 11           LDA #$11
4039 20 D2 FF        JSR $FFD2
403C A9 9D           LDA #$9D
403E 20 D2 FF        JSR $FFD2
4041 A9 94           LDA #$94
```

53

```
4043 20 D2 FF    JSR $FFD2
4046 A9 80       LDA #$80
4048 85 DA       STA $DA
404A 60          RTS
404B 00          BRK
```

Scrolling to the left and the right works in exactly the same way as the up and down scroll, except that we are using register 53270. Here is the pixel scroll routine for left.

```
1000 AD 16 D0    LDA $D016
1003 29 F8       AND #$F8
1005 18          CLC
1006 6D 5B 10    ADC $105B
1009 8D 16 D0    STA $D016
100C CE 5B 10    DEC $105B
100F AD 5B 10    LDA $105B
1012 C9 FF       CMP #$FF
1014 F0 01       BEQ $1017
1016 60          RTS
1017 AD 16 D0    LDA $D016
101A 29 F8       AND #$F8
101C 18          CLC
101D 69 07       ADC #$07
101F 8D 16 D0    STA $D016
1022 A9 07       LDA #$07
1024 8D 5B 10    STA $105B
1027 20 2B 10    JSR $102B
102A 60          RTS
102B A9 06       LDA #$06
102D 8D 44 03    STA $0344
1030 A2 00       LDX #$00
1032 A0 00       LDY #$00
1034 BD 01 04    LDA $0401,X
1037 9D 00 04    STA $0400,X
103A BD F1 04    LDA $04F1,X
103D 9D F0 04    STA $04F0,X
1040 BD E1 05    LDA $05E1,X
1043 9D E0 05    STA $05E0,X
1046 BD D1 06    LDA $06D1,X
```

54

```
1049 9D DØ Ø6    STA $Ø6DØ,X
1Ø4C E8          INX
1Ø4D C8          INY
1Ø4E CØ 27       CPY #$27
1Ø5Ø DØ E2       BNE $1Ø34
1Ø52 E8          INX
1Ø53 AØ ØØ       LDY #$ØØ
1Ø55 CE 44 Ø3    DEC $Ø344
1Ø58 DØ DA       BNE $1Ø34
1Ø5A 6Ø          RTS
1Ø5B Ø7          ???
```

The right pixel scroll is exactly the same as the left scroll, except that we increment the counter to eight rather than decrement it to #$FF. Here is the pixel right scroll. It uses the same scroll routine as in the previous right character scroll routine to show how they may be combined.

```
1ØØØ AD 16 DØ    LDA $DØ16
1ØØ3 29 F8       AND #$F8
1ØØ5 18          CLC
1ØØ6 6D C9 1Ø    ADC $1ØC9
1ØØ9 8D 16 DØ    STA $DØ16
1ØØC EE C9 1Ø    INC $1ØC9
1ØØF AD C9 1Ø    LDA $1ØC9
1Ø12 C9 Ø8       CMP #$Ø8
1Ø14 FØ Ø1       BEQ $1Ø17
1Ø16 6Ø          RTS
1Ø17 A9 ØØ       LDA #$ØØ
1Ø19 8D C9 1Ø    STA $1ØC9
1Ø1C AD 16 DØ    LDA $DØ16
1Ø1F 29 F8       AND #$F8
1Ø21 8D 16 DØ    STA $DØ16
1Ø24 2Ø 28 1Ø    JSR $1Ø28
1Ø27 6Ø          RTS
1Ø28 A2 26       LDX #$26
1Ø2A BD ØØ Ø4    LDA $Ø4ØØ,X
1Ø2D 9D Ø1 Ø4    STA $Ø4Ø1,X
1Ø3Ø BD 28 Ø4    LDA $Ø428,X
1Ø33 9D 29 Ø4    STA $Ø429,X
1Ø36 BD 5Ø Ø4    LDA $Ø45Ø,X
```

```
1039 9D 51 04      STA $0451,X
103C BD 78 04      LDA $0478,X
103F 9D 79 04      STA $0479,X
1042 BD A0 04      LDA $04A0,X
1045 9D A1 04      STA $04A1,X
1048 BD C8 04      LDA $04C8,X
104B 9D C9 04      STA $04C9,X
104E BD F0 04      LDA $04F0,X
1051 9D F1 04      STA $04F1,X
1054 BD 18 05      LDA $0518,X
1057 9D 19 05      STA $0519,X
105A BD 40 05      LDA $0540,X
105D 9D 41 05      STA $0541,X
1060 BD 68 05      LDA $0568,X
1063 9D 69 05      STA $0569,X
1066 BD 90 05      LDA $0590,X
1069 9D 91 05      STA $0591,X
106C BD B8 05      LDA $05B8,X
106F 9D B9 05      STA $05B9,X
1072 BD E0 05      LDA $05E0,X
1075 9D E1 05      STA $05E1,X
1078 BD 08 06      LDA $0608,X
107B 9D 09 06      STA $0609,X
107E BD 30 06      LDA $0630,X
1081 9D 31 06      STA $0631,X
1084 BD 58 06      LDA $0658,X
1087 9D 59 06      STA $0659,X
108A BD 80 06      LDA $0680,X
108D 9D 81 06      STA $0681,X
1090 BD A8 06      LDA $06A8,X
1093 9D A9 06      STA $06A9,X
1096 BD D0 06      LDA $06D0,X
1099 9D D1 06      STA $06D1,X
109C BD F8 06      LDA $06F8,X
109F 9D F9 06      STA $06F9,X
10A2 BD 20 07      LDA $0720,X
10A5 9D 21 07      STA $0721,X
10A8 BD 48 07      LDA $0748,X
10AB 9D 49 07      STA $0749,X
10AE BD 70 07      LDA $0770,X
```

```
10B1 9D 71 07      STA $0771,X
10B4 BD 98 07      LDA $0798,X
10B7 9D 99 07      STA $0799,X
10BA BD C0 07      LDA $07C0,X
10BD 9D C1 07      STA $07C1,X
10C0 CA            DEX
10C1 E0 FF         CPX #$FF
10C3 F0 03         BEQ $10C8
10C5 4C 2A 10      JMP $102A
10C8 60            RTS
10C9 00            BRK
     .
```

SPRITES

Sprites can be moved at a reasonable speed in BASIC, but for any arcade game it is just too slow. Here is a program that allows you to move a sprite (Sprite 2) about the screen using the following keys:

F1 = up

F7 = down

A = left

D = right

To use the program, SYS 7172 from BASIC or JSR $1C04 from machine code.

```
1CØØ  4C A9 1C      JMP $1CA9
1CØ3  EA            NOP
1CØ4  A5 C5         LDA $C5
1CØ6  C9 12         CMP #$12
1CØ8  FØ 11         BEQ $1C1B
1CØA  C9 ØA         CMP #$ØA
1CØC  FØ 46         BEQ $1C54
1CØE  C9 Ø4         CMP #$Ø4
1C10  FØ 7B         BEQ $1C8D
1C12  C9 Ø3         CMP #$Ø3
1C14  FØ EA         BEQ $1CØØ
1C16  EA            NOP
1C17  EA            NOP
1C18  EA            NOP
1C19  EA            NOP
1C1A  6Ø            RTS
1C1B  A8            TAY
1C1C  AD 10 DØ      LDA $DØ10
1C1F  29 Ø4         AND #$Ø4
1C21  C9 Ø4         CMP #$Ø4
```

```
1C23 FØ ØF        BEQ $1C34
1C25 AE Ø4 DØ     LDX $DØØ4
1C28 EØ FF        CPX #$FF
1C2A FØ 17        BEQ $1C43
1C2C E8           INX
1C2D 8E Ø4 DØ     STX $DØØ4
1C3Ø 98           TYA
1C31 4C 16 1C     JMP $1C16
1C34 AE Ø4 DØ     LDX $DØØ4
1C37 EØ 3F        CPX #$3F
1C39 FØ Ø4        BEQ $1C3F
1C3B E8           INX
1C3C 8E Ø4 DØ     STX $DØØ4
1C3F 98           TYA
1C4Ø 4C 16 1C     JMP $1C16
1C43 AD 1Ø DØ     LDA $DØ1Ø
1C46 Ø9 Ø4        ORA #$Ø4
1C48 8D 1Ø DØ     STA $DØ1Ø
1C4B A2 ØØ        LDX #$ØØ
1C4D 8E Ø4 DØ     STX $DØØ4
1C5Ø 98           TYA
1C51 4C 16 1C     JMP $1C16
1C54 A8           TAY
1C55 AD 1Ø DØ     LDA $DØ1Ø
1C58 29 Ø4        AND #$Ø4
1C5A C9 Ø4        CMP #$Ø4
1C5C FØ ØF        BEQ $1C6D
1C5E AE Ø4 DØ     LDX $DØØ4
1C61 EØ 16        CPX #$16
1C63 FØ Ø4        BEQ $1C69
1C65 CA           DEX
1C66 8E Ø4 DØ     STX $DØØ4
1C69 98           TYA
1C6A 4C 16 1C     JMP $1C16
1C6D AE Ø4 DØ     LDX $DØØ4
1C7Ø EØ ØØ        CPX #$ØØ
1C72 FØ Ø8        BEQ $1C7C
1C74 CA           DEX
1C75 8E Ø4 DØ     STX $DØØ4
1C78 98           TYA
```

```
1C79 4C 16 1C      JMP $1C16
1C7C AD 10 D0      LDA $D010
1C7F 29 FB         AND #$FB
1C81 8D 10 D0      STA $D010
1C84 A2 FF         LDX #$FF
1C86 8E 04 D0      STX $D004
1C89 98            TYA
1C8A 4C 16 1C      JMP $1C16
1C8D AE 05 D0      LDX $D005
1C90 E0 2E         CPX #$2E
1C92 F0 11         BEQ $1CA5
1C94 AD 1E D0      LDA $D01E
1C97 29 04         AND #$04
1C99 C9 04         CMP #$04
1C9B D0 04         BNE $1CA1
1C9D 98            TYA
1C9E 4C 16 1C      JMP $1C16
1CA1 CA            DEX
1CA2 8E 05 D0      STX $D005
1CA5 98            TYA
1CA6 4C 16 1C      JMP $1C16
1CA9 AE 05 D0      LDX $D005
1CAC E0 ED         CPX #$ED
1CAE F0 0D         BEQ $1CBD
1CB0 AD 1E D0      LDA $D01E
1CB3 29 04         AND #$04
1CB5 C9 04         CMP #$04
1CB7 F0 04         BEQ $1CBD
1CB9 E8            INX
1CBA 8E 05 D0      STX $D005
1CBD 98            TYA
1CBE 4C 16 1C      JMP $1C16
```

If you are using sprites in a program, the time will come when
you want to find what character the sprite is under or over.
(You might be able to see which one, but the computer can't!
Commodore kindly made it possible for the Video chip to
detect if it has hit a character or not, but not to detect which
one.) The following program does this—it is written to detect
the character under Sprite 0. To find out which character it is,

use SYS 16384 from BASIC or JSR $4000 from machine code. The character code is returned in location 828 ($033C)—so to find out the character execute the routine and PEEK or LDA (X or Y) location 828 ($033C).

```
.
4000  AD 00 D0      LDA $D000
4003  38            SEC
4004  E9 18         SBC #$18
4006  AA            TAX
4007  AD 10 D0      LDA $D010
400A  C9 01         CMP #$01
400C  D0 03         BNE $4011
400E  AE 00 D0      LDX $D000
4011  AD 01 D0      LDA $D001
4014  38            SEC
4015  E9 3A         SBC #$3A
4017  A8            TAY
4018  8E 98 40      STX $4098
401B  8C 9A 40      STY $409A
401E  98            TYA
401F  4A            LSR
4020  4A            LSR
4021  4A            LSR
4022  18            CLC
4023  69 01         ADC #$01
4025  8D 9B 40      STA $409B
4028  8A            TXA
4029  4A            LSR
402A  4A            LSR
402B  4A            LSR
402C  8D 99 40      STA $4099
402F  AD 10 D0      LDA $D010
4032  C9 01         CMP #$01
4034  D0 09         BNE $403F
4036  AD 99 40      LDA $4099
4039  18            CLC
403A  69 1D         ADC #$1D
403C  8D 99 40      STA $4099
403F  AD 9B 40      LDA $409B
4042  8D 96 40      STA $4096
4045  A9 28         LDA #$28
```

```
4047 8D 97 40    STA $4097
404A 20 79 40    JSR $4079
404D AD 99 40    LDA $4099
4050 6D 94 40    ADC $4094
4053 8D 94 40    STA $4094
4056 AD 95 40    LDA $4095
4059 69 00       ADC #$00
405B 8D 95 40    STA $4095
405E AD 95 40    LDA $4095
4061 18          CLC
4062 69 04       ADC #$04
4064 8D 95 40    STA $4095
4067 AD 94 40    LDA $4094
406A 85 FB       STA $FB
406C AD 95 40    LDA $4095
406F 85 FC       STA $FC
4071 A0 00       LDY #$00
4073 B1 FB       LDA ($FB),Y
4075 8D 3C 03    STA $033C
4078 60          RTS
4079 A9 00       LDA #$00
407B 8D 94 40    STA $4094
407E A2 08       LDX #$08
4080 4E 96 40    LSR $4096
4083 90 04       BCC $4089
4085 18          CLC
4086 6D 97 40    ADC $4097
4089 6A          ROR
408A 6E 94 40    ROR $4094
408D CA          DEX
408E D0 F0       BNE $4080
4090 8D 95 40    STA $4095
4093 60          RTS
4094 00          BRK
4095 00          BRK
4096 00          BRK
4097 00          BRK
4098 00          BRK
4099 00          BRK
409A 00          BRK
409B 00          BRK
  .
```

No doubt you will want to check which character is under a different sprite to Sprite 0. Rather than listing eight programs, one for each sprite, here is a list of what to change to make it work for any sprite.

1: Change the first line from LDA $D000 to LDA $XXXX (where 'XXXX' is the Hex location of the X co-ordinate of the sprite that you want to test).

2: Change the line at address $400A to CMP #SXXXX (where 'XXXX' is the bit value of the sprite to be tested (Sprite 0=1 through to Sprite 7=128).

3: Change the line at address $400E to LDX $XXXX (where 'XXXX' is the Hex location of the X co-ordinate of the sprite to be tested).

4: Change the line at address $4011 to LDA $XXXX (where 'XXXX' is the Hex location of the Y co-ordinate of the sprite to be tested).

5: Change the line at address $4032 to CMP #$XXXX (where 'XXXX' is the bit value of the sprite to be tested.

The routine checks which character is under the top left eight bytes of the sprite (going down). For example:

```
1  2  3
1  2  3
1  2  3
1  2  3
1  2  3
1  2  3
1  2  3
1  2  3
```

and so on . . . It checks the character under the 1s in the above diagram. However, this can be altered by changing two bytes in the program as follows.

The line at location $4004 is SBC #$18. The number after the SBC must never be less than $18 (24), but if you add one to this value for every bit across the sprite then you can alter where on the horizontal the routine will check. (This number must never exceed $30 (48) if the sprite is not expanded in the X direction or $60 (96) if expanded.) Remember that if the sprite is expanded, each dot on the sprite is two dots wide, and therefore you will need to multiply the amount greater than $18 by two and add it to $18, e.g. to get the routine to check for the rightmost eight bits of an unexpanded sprite make the line SBC #$30. Or, to get the routine to check for the last seven bits to the 15th bit across in an expanded sprite, make the line SBC #(24+7*2) which is SBC #$26.

To alter where the routine checks on the vertical, change the line at address $4015 (SBC #$3A). The rules for changing are the same as for the X direction. If the sprite is unexpanded in the Y direction then the value is $3A plus the byte down. If the sprite is expanded then the value is $3A plus twice the byte down. The value must never be less than $3A (and if the sprite is unexpanded, no greater than $4f (79) or if the sprite is expanded, no greater than $64 (100)) for the routine to give the correct result, e.g. to make the routine check for the botton eight bytes of the sprite when it is unexpanded, the line is SBC #$47. Or to make the routine check for the 10th to the 18th byte down in an expanded sprite, the line is SBC #$3A plus 2*10 which is SBC #$4E.

MUSIC

All of the following programs to demonstrate sound and music are in two parts: first the machine code and then the data for the scale or tunes. Both are required to be typed in. Then to save the program, you must save from the start location of the machine code to the last data number inclusive. (The last data number is included to fill space so that the SAVE command in *SUPERMON* works correctly.)

Sound is easy to access in machine code—all it requires is a straight conversion of the POKEs in BASIC. The following program plays a scale using one sound channel:

```
·
8000 A9 0F          LDA #$0F
8002 8D 18 D4        STA $D418
8005 A9 38          LDA #$38
8007 8D 05 D4        STA $D405
800A 8D 06 D4        STA $D406
800D A9 21          LDA #$21
800F 8D 04 D4        STA $D404
8012 A2 00          LDX #$00
8014 BD 39 80        LDA $8039,X
8017 8D 00 D4        STA $D400
801A BD 3A 80        LDA $803A,X
801D 8D 01 D4        STA $D401
8020 8A             TXA
8021 48             PHA
8022 A2 00          LDX #$00
8024 A0 00          LDY #$00
8026 E8             INX
8027 D0 FD          BNE $8026
8029 C8             INY
802A C0 A0          CPY #$A0
802C 90 F8          BCC $8026
802E 68             PLA
802F AA             TAX
```

65

```
8030 E8            INX
8031 E8            INX
8032 E0 24         CPX #$24
8034 90 DE         BCC $8014
8036 D0 DC         BNE $8014
8038 60            RTS
    .
    .
    .
    .
.:8039 4B 22 7E 26 34 2B C6 2D
.:8041 61 33 AC 39 BC 40 95 44
.:8049 00 00 95 44 BC 40 AC 39
.:8051 61 33 C6 2D 34 2B 7E 26
.:8059 4B 22 00 00 FF FF FF 00
    .
```

It can be seen from the above program, all that is being done is the reading of data stored in memory directly after the program. This data is then stored in the registers for channel one (54272,3).

The same method can be used to play a tune. The only difference is that we must have data in memory for the delay between notes. The following program demonstrates this:

```
    .
8000 A9 0F         LDA #$0F
8002 8D 18 D4      STA $D418
8005 A9 38         LDA #$38
8007 8D 05 D4      STA $D405
800A 8D 06 D4      STA $D406
800D A9 21         LDA #$21
800F 8D 04 D4      STA $D404
8012 A2 00         LDX #$00
8014 A0 00         LDY #$00
8016 BD 3E 80      LDA $803E,X
8019 8D 00 D4      STA $D400
801C BD 3F 80      LDA $803F,X
801F 8D 01 D4      STA $D401
8022 8A            TXA
```

66

```
8023 48          PHA
8024 98          TYA
8025 48          PHA
8026 B9 70 80    LDA $8070,Y
8029 A2 00       LDX #$00
802B A8          TAY
802C E8          INX
802D D0 FD       BNE $802C
802F 88          DEY
8030 D0 FA       BNE $802C
8032 68          PLA
8033 A8          TAY
8034 68          PLA
8035 AA          TAX
8036 E8          INX
8037 E8          INX
8038 C8          INY
8039 E0 30       CPX #$30
803B 90 D9       BCC $8016
803D 60          RTS
  .
  .
  .
  .
.:803E 95 44 00 00 95 44 BC 40
.:8046 AC 39 00 00 AC 39 61 33
.:804E AC 39 61 33 C6 2D 34 2B
.:8056 00 00 34 2B C6 2D 61 33
.:805E 4B 22 7E 26 C6 2D 34 2B
.:8066 7E 26 4B 22 00 00 00 00
.:806E 00 00 C8 C8 C8 FF FF FA
.:8076 FF E1 FA FF DC DC DC FF
.:807E E6 FF FF FF FF FF FF FF
.:8086 FF 7F FF FF 7D FF FF FF
```

To make music in three channels is just as easy. The following program plays the above scale in three voices. Rather than using three different sets of data for the notes I have added 10 ($0A) to the note value for Voice 2 and 20 ($14) to Voice 3. This gives a much more deep sound than that with Voice 1 but makes the sound a little bit flat.

.

```
8000 A9 0F        LDA #$0F
8002 8D 18 D4     STA $D418
8005 A9 38        LDA #$38
8007 8D 05 D4     STA $D405
800A 8D 0C D4     STA $D40C
800D 8D 13 D4     STA $D413
8010 8D 06 D4     STA $D406
8013 8D 0D D4     STA $D40D
8016 8D 14 D4     STA $D414
8019 A9 21        LDA #$21
801B A2 13        LDX #$13
801D 8D 04 D4     STA $D404
8020 8D 0B D4     STA $D40B
8023 8E 12 D4     STX $D412
8026 A2 00        LDX #$00
8028 BD 79 80     LDA $8079,X
802B 8D 00 D4     STA $D400
802E 69 0A        ADC #$0A
8030 8D 07 D4     STA $D407
8033 69 0A        ADC #$0A
8035 8D 0E D4     STA $D40E
8038 BD 7A 80     LDA $807A,X
803B 8D 01 D4     STA $D401
803E 69 0B        ADC #$0B
8040 8D 08 D4     STA $D408
8043 69 0B        ADC #$0B
8045 8D 0F D4     STA $D40F
8048 8A           TXA
8049 48           PHA
804A 98           TYA
804B 48           PHA
804C A2 00        LDX #$00
804E A0 00        LDY #$00
8050 E8           INX
8051 D0 FD        BNE $8050
8053 C8           INY
8054 C0 A0        CPY #$A0
8056 90 F8        BCC $8050
8058 68           PLA
8059 A8           TAY
```

```
805A 68              PLA
805B AA              TAX
805C E8              INX
805D E8              INX
805E E0 24           CPX #$24
8060 90 C6           BCC $8028
8062 D0 C4           BNE $8028
8064 A9 00           LDA #$00
8066 8D 00 D4        STA $D400
8069 8D 01 D4        STA $D401
806C 8D 07 D4        STA $D407
806F 8D 08 D4        STA $D408
8072 8D 0E D4        STA $D40E
8075 8D 0F D4        STA $D40F
8078 60              RTS
.
.
.
.:8079 4B 22 7E 26 34 2B C6 2D
.:8081 61 33 AC 39 BC 40 95 44
.:8089 00 00 95 44 BC 40 AC 39
.:8091 61 33 C6 2D 34 2B 7E 26
.:8099 4B 22 00 00 FF FF FF 00
.
```

The same method can be used for playing tunes in three
channels. However, the following program plays to different
musical parts—Voice 1 plays the lead and Voices 2 and 3
play the same tune in harmony. Voice 1 has a coarse sound
created by the sawtooth waveform, Voice 2 has a triangle
waveform and Voice 3 again has a sawtooth waveform.

```
.
8000 A9 0F           LDA #$0F
8002 8D 18 D4        STA $D418
8005 A9 38           LDA #$38
8007 8D 05 D4        STA $D405
800A 8D 0C D4        STA $D40C
800D 8D 13 D4        STA $D413
8010 8D 06 D4        STA $D406
8013 8D 0D D4        STA $D40D
8016 8D 14 D4        STA $D414
```

69

```
8019 A9 21        LDA #$21
801B 8D 04 D4     STA $D404
801E A9 13        LDA #$13
8020 8D 01 D4     STA $D401
8023 A9 21        LDA #$21
8025 8D 12 D4     STA $D412
8028 A2 00        LDX #$00
802A A0 00        LDY #$00
802C BD 7D 80     LDA $807D,X
802F 8D 00 D4     STA $D400
8032 BD B1 80     LDA $80B1,X
8035 8D 07 D4     STA $D407
8038 8D 0E D4     STA $D40E
803B BD 7E 80     LDA $807E,X
803E 8D 01 D4     STA $D401
8041 BD B2 80     LDA $80B2,X
8044 8D 08 D4     STA $D408
8047 8D 0F D4     STA $D40F
804A 8A           TXA
804B 48           PHA
804C 98           TYA
804D 48           PHA
804E B9 66 80     LDA $8066,Y
8051 A2 00        LDX #$00
8053 A8           TAY
8054 E8           INX
8055 D0 FD        BNE $8054
8057 88           DEY
8058 D0 FA        BNE $8054
805A 68           PLA
805B A8           TAY
805C 68           PLA
805D AA           TAX
805E E8           INX
805F E8           INX
8060 C8           INY
8061 E0 30        CPX #$30
8063 90 C7        BCC $802C
8065 60           RTS
```
.

```
.
.:8066 C8 C8 C8 FF FF FA FF E1
.:806E FA FF DC DC DC FF E6 FF
.:8076 FF FF FF FF FF FF FF C6
.:807E 2D 00 00 C6 2D 34 2B 7E
.:8086 26 00 00 7E 26 4B 22 7E
.:808E 26 4B 22 8D 1E D6 1C 00
.:8096 00 D6 1C 8D 1E 4B 22 E3
.:809E 16 B1 19 8D 1E D6 1C B1
.:80A6 19 E3 16 00 00 00 00 00
.:80AE 00 00 00 72 0B 00 00 72
.:80B6 0B CD 0A 9F 09 00 00 9F
.:80BE 09 93 08 9F 09 93 08 A3
.:80C6 07 35 07 00 00 35 07 A3
.:80CE 07 93 08 B9 05 6C 06 A3
.:80D6 07 35 07 6C 06 B9 05 00
.:80DE 00 00 00 00 00 00 00 00
.
```

INTERRUPTS

Interrupts are one of the things that a computer can only do in machine code. They occur every 60th of a second and happen whether the computer is doing something or not—even when RUNning a BASIC or machine code program. This happens with all computers and microprocessors, but on the '64 they are specifically used to update the clock, read the keyboard and various other 'housekeeping' functions. Most interesting is the fact that an interrupt can be interrupted and a function can be added to it.

There are two main types of interrupt: the IRQ (interrupt request) and the NMI (non-maskable interrupt). The latter is used for the operating system and is not practical for use in our programs. The other, IRQ, is a two-byte vector through which a routine is called by the JMP (address) command in machine code. The way that we intercept this vector is to change the address contained in the vector.

The vector is addresses 788 ($0314) and 789 ($0315). The address that will be jumped to is contained in 788 and 789 in lo-byte hi-byte format, i.e. if the address was 4096 ($1000), location 789 would contain 16 ($10) which is 4096/256. Location 788 would contain the remainder of the above division multiplied by 256. Here is another example—to make the jump address 65490, divide 65490 by 256:

65490/256=255.8203125

So location 789 (the hi-byte) would contain 255. The remainder is .8203125, so multiply that by 256:

.8203125*256=210

So location 788 (the lo-byte) would contain 210.
The computer would now jump to 65490 ($ffd2) every 60th of a second. *Don't* try it as the computer will crash—this is only an example.

When we are changing an interrupt, if either the lo-byte or hi-byte are altered when an interrupt is being called the computer will probably crash. We must therefore turn them off while we change the vector. This is done with the command 'SEI' (which means SEt Interrupt disable flag). When this command is encountered in a machine code program by the processor it stops all IRQ interrupts until the bit is cleared with the CLI command (CLear Interrupt disable flag). This can only be done with IRQ as the NMI is unstoppable.

There is one other essential thing that you must do when changing an interrupt. When your routine has finished its work, it must jump to location $EA31 by making the last command JMP $EA31 (instead of RTS or RTI).

The following program demonstrates the use of interrupts. It increments the border colour every 60th of a second. Not very great you say—I know, but it serves to illustrate the point.

```
.
7000 78              SEI
7001 A9 0D           LDA #$0D
7003 8D 14 03        STA $0314
7006 A9 70           LDA #$70
7008 8D 15 03        STA $0315
700B 58              CLI
700C 60              RTS
700D EE 20 D0        INC $D020
7010 4C 31 EA        JMP $EA31
.
```

As you may have noticed when you have tried to use the function keys on the '64, they don't work! Well, that is not strictly true because they do, except that Commodore never provided software in ROM for using them. We may want these keys to print a keyword, for example, whenever we hit a function key. The best way to achieve that is to intercept the keyboard scan routine and do our own check for these

73

keys and this can be achieved using the IRQ interrupt. The following program does just that:

```
.
C000 78            SEI
C001 A9 10         LDA #$10
C003 8D 14 03      STA $0314
C006 A9 C0         LDA #$C0
C008 8D 15 03      STA $0315
C00B 58            CLI
C00C 60            RTS
C00D EA            NOP
C00E EA            NOP
C00F EA            NOP
C010 48            PHA
C011 8A            TXA
C012 48            PHA
C013 98            TYA
C014 48            PHA
C015 A5 C5         LDA $C5
C017 C5 FB         CMP $FB
C019 F0 51         BEQ $C06C
C01B 85 FB         STA $FB
C01D C9 03         CMP #$03
C01F D0 08         BNE $C029
C021 A9 30         LDA #$30
C023 8D 00 C1      STA $C100
C026 4C 4A C0      JMP $C04A
C029 C9 04         CMP #$04
C02B D0 08         BNE $C035
C02D A9 00         LDA #$00
C02F 8D 00 C1      STA $C100
C032 4C 4A C0      JMP $C04A
C035 C9 05         CMP #$05
C037 D0 08         BNE $C041
C039 A9 10         LDA #$10
C03B 8D 00 C1      STA $C100
C03E 4C 4A C0      JMP $C04A
C041 C9 06         CMP #$06
C043 D0 27         BNE $C06C
C045 A9 20         LDA #$20
```

```
C047 8D 00 C1        STA $C100
C04A AD 8D 02        LDA $028D
C04D C9 01           CMP #$01
C04F D0 08           BNE $C059
C051 AD 00 C1        LDA $C100
C054 69 08           ADC #$08
C056 8D 00 C1        STA $C100
C059 A2 00           LDX #$00
C05B AC 00 C1        LDY $C100
C05E B9 01 C1        LDA $C101,Y
C061 9D 77 02        STA $0277,X
C064 E8              INX
C065 C8              INY
C066 E0 08           CPX #$08
C068 D0 F4           BNE $C05E
C06A 86 C6           STX $C6
C06C 68              PLA
C06D A8              TAY
C06E 68              PLA
C06F AA              TAX
C070 68              PLA
C071 4C 31 EA        JMP $EA31
.
```

The above program needs data for the letters to put on the
keys. Therefore, the best way to enter the program is to use a
BASIC loader. The following program is just that. The '/'
characters are to fill space in the quotes as each command
must be eight characters in length. The back arrow is used to
put a carriage return onto the keys. To put different words
onto the keys just change what is inside the quotes, but
make sure that you don't exceed eight characters, or if you
use less fill the rest with '/' characters.

```
10 DATA 120,169,16,141,20,3,169,192,141,
21,3,88,96,234,234,234,72,138,72,152,72
15 DATA 165,197,197,251,240,81,133,251,2
01,3,208,8,169,48,141,0,193,76,74,192
20 DATA201,4,208,8,169,0,141,0,193,76,74
,192,201,5,208,8,169,16,141,0,193,76,74
25 DATA 192,201,6,208,39,169,32,141,0,19
```

```
  3,173,141,2,201,1,208,8,173,0,193,105,8
30 DATA141,0,193,162,0,172,0,193,185,1,1
93,157,119,2,232,200,224,8,208,244,134
35 DATA198,104,168,104,170,104,76,49,234

40 FORA=49152T049267:READB:POKEA,B:NEXT
50 FORA=0T07:READK$:FORB=1T08:L=ASC((MID
$(K$,B,1))):IFL=95THENL=13
55 IFL=47THENL=4
60 POKE49409+(A*8)+B,L:NEXT:NEXT:POKE494
09,4:SYS49152
70 DATA"LIST←///"
80 DATA"PRINT///"
90 DATA"RUN←////"
100 DATA"THEN////"
110 DATA"LOAD////"
120 DATA"SAVE////"
130 DATA"VERIFY//"
140 DATA"GOTO////"
```

The above method can be used to program the rest of the keyboard to make one key entries as employed on the ZX range of computers possible. The following program does just that; however, the keys '1'–'0','q','s','m','CRSR right' and 'down', and a few other keys cannot be used due to the fact that they produce control codes that cannot be stopped easily.

The program and the monitor dump should be typed in first and saved as the program after them contains the data required to put onto the keys, and it is easier to read and change the data in data statements than a monitor display. The monitor dump is the data for the keyboard that the program requires before it will work.

The maximum number of characters that can be put on each key is four. To start the program, load the machine code into memory using the 'LOAD"name",device,1' instruction from BASIC or 'L"name",device (01,08)' from *SUPER-MON*. Then you will need to load and RUN the data program and type SYS 32768.

```
  .
  .
8000 78              SEI
8001 A9 0D           LDA #$0D
8003 8D 14 03        STA $0314
8006 A9 80           LDA #$80
8008 8D 15 03        STA $0315
800B 58              CLI
800C 60              RTS
800D 48              PHA
800E 8A              TXA
800F 48              PHA
8010 98              TYA
8011 48              PHA
8012 A5 C5           LDA $C5
8014 C5 FB           CMP $FB
8016 D0 08           BNE $8020
8018 68              PLA
8019 A8              TAY
801A 68              PLA
801B AA              TAX
801C 68              PLA
801D 4C 31 EA        JMP $EA31
8020 85 FB           STA $FB
8022 AD 8D 02        LDA $028D
8025 C9 04           CMP #$04
8027 D0 EF           BNE $8018
8029 A2 00           LDX #$00
802B BD 57 80        LDA $8057,X
802E C5 FB           CMP $FB
8030 F0 08           BEQ $803A
8032 E8              INX
8033 E0 25           CPX #$25
8035 D0 F4           BNE $802B
8037 4C 18 80        JMP $8018
803A 86 FC           STX $FC
803C 8A              TXA
803D 0A              ASL
803E 0A              ASL
803F 85 FC           STA $FC
8041 AA              TAX
```

```
8042 A6 FC          LDX $FC
8044 AØ ØØ          LDY #$ØØ
8046 BD 8D 8Ø       LDA $8Ø8D,X
8049 99 77 Ø2       STA $Ø277,Y
8Ø4C C8             INY
8Ø4D E8             INX
8Ø4E CØ Ø4          CPY #$Ø4
8Ø5Ø DØ F4          BNE $8Ø46
8Ø52 84 C6          STY $C6
8Ø54 4C 18 8Ø       JMP $8Ø18
     .

     .
.:8Ø57 39 28 2B 33 ØØ Ø9 ØE 11
.:8Ø5F 19 1E 21 26 29 2E ØA 12
.:8Ø67 15 1A 1D 22 25 2A 2D Ø1
.:8Ø6F ØC 17 14 1F 1C 27 2F 2C
.:8Ø77 37 Ø4 Ø5 Ø6 Ø3 FF C6 2D
```

In the following listing, '_' is the left arrow which stands for
a carriage return and '∧' is an up arrow (a character to fill
space).

```
10 fora=Øto59:reada$
20 forb=1to4:b$=mid$(a$,b,1):ifb$="^"the
nb$=chr$(Ø)
30 ifb$="_"thenb$=chr$(13)
40 poke32909+a*4+b-1,asc(b$):b$="":next:
next
100 data"let^"
110 data"peek"
120 data"poke"
130 data"load"
140 data"save"
150 data"ve^^"
160 data"stop"
170 data"for^"
180 data"next"
190 data"read"
200 data"reT^"
210 data"run_"
```

```
220 data"lI_^"
230 data"list"
240 data"run^"
250 data"if^^"
260 data"then"
270 data"goto"
280 data"goS^"
290 data"wait"
300 data"?pE("
310 data"on^^"
320 data"chr$"
330 data"asc("
340 data"fre("
350 data"sin("
360 data"cos("
370 data"tan("
380 data"atn("
390 data"sys^"
400 data"usr("
410 data"open"
420 data"clO^"
430 data"iN^^"
440 data"get^"
450 data"clr^"
460 data"cmd^"
470 data"cont"
480 data"def^"
490 data"dim^"
500 data"end^"
510 data"reT^"
520 data"and^"
530 data"rnd("
540 data"sqr("
550 data"step"
560 data"tab("
570 data"val^"
580 data"not^"
590 data"exp^"
600 data"vE^^"
610 data"vE_^"
```

```
620 data"for^"
630 data"next"
640 data"read"
650 data"res^"
660 data"run_"
670 data"1I_^"
680 data"list"
690 data"run^"
```

The IRQ can be used for much less serious routines. The following program plays a tune throughout the interrupt; it plays two musical parts, one of them starting after the other. If you listen carefully you notice that they both play the same tune, but with different waveforms and pitch.

```
        .
8000 78              sei
8001 a9 32           lda #$32
8003 8d 14 03        sta $0314
8006 a9 80           lda #$80
8008 8d 15 03        sta $0315
800b a9 0f           lda #$0f
800d 8d 18 d4        sta $d418
8010 a9 13           lda #$13
8012 8d 04 d4        sta $d404
8015 a9 40           lda #$40
8017 8d 05 d4        sta $d405
801a 8d 06 d4        sta $d406
801d 8d 0c d4        sta $d40c
8020 8d 0d d4        sta $d40d
8023 a9 21           lda #$21
8025 8d 0b d4        sta $d40b
8028 a9 00           lda #$00
802a 85 fb           sta $fb
802c 85 fc           sta $fc
802e 85 fd           sta $fd
8030 58              cli
8031 60              rts
8032 a6 fb           ldx $fb
8034 a4 fc           ldy $fc
8036 bd 74 80        lda $8074,x
```

80

```
8039 8d 00 d4    sta $d400
803c bd a6 80    lda $80a6,x
803f 8d 07 d4    sta $d407
8042 bd a7 80    lda $80a7,x
8045 8d 08 d4    sta $d408
8048 bd 75 80    lda $8075,x
804b 8d 01 d4    sta $d401
804e a5 fd       lda $fd
8050 c9 0a       cmp #$0a
8052 b0 05       bcs $8059
8054 e6 fd       inc $fd
8056 4c 31 ea    jmp $ea31
8059 a9 00       lda #$00
805b 85 fd       sta $fd
805d e8          inx
805e e8          inx
805f c8          iny
8060 86 fb       stx $fb
8062 84 fc       sty $fc
8064 e0 30       cpx #$30
8066 b0 03       bcs $806b
8068 4c 31 ea    jmp $ea31
806b a2 00       ldx #$00
806d 85 fb       sta $fb
806f 85 fc       sta $fc
8071 4c 31 ea    jmp $ea31
     .
.:8074 c6 2d 00 00 c6 2d 34 2b
.:807c 7e 26 00 00 7e 26 4b 22
.:8084 7e 26 4b 22 8d 1e d6 1c
.:808c 00 00 d6 1c 8d 1e 4b 22
.:8094 e3 16 b1 19 8d 1e d6 1c
.:809c b1 19 e3 16 00 00 00 00
.:80a4 00 00 00 00 72 0b 00 00
.:80ac 72 0b cd 0a 9f 09 00 00
.:80b4 9f 09 93 08 9f 09 93 08
.:80bc a3 07 35 07 00 00 35 07
.:80c4 a3 07 93 08 b9 05 6c 06
.:80cc a3 07 35 07 6c 06 b9 05
.:80d4 00 00 00 00 00 00 00 00
```

Still on a musical note (sorry!), here is an interrupt driven program that allows you to use the second row of keys on the keyboard as a simple organ. The notes are not stored but the program could be extended to do this easily. The keys used are:

QWERTYUIOP@ *

and the space bar is used to give a space, i.e. it turns off the music.

```
.
C000 78              SEI
C001 A9 1F           LDA #$1F
C003 8D 14 03        STA $0314
C006 A9 C0           LDA #$C0
C008 8D 15 03        STA $0315
C00B A9 0F           LDA #$0F
C00D 8D 18 D4        STA $D418
C010 A9 21           LDA #$21
C012 8D 04 D4        STA $D404
C015 A9 38           LDA #$38
C017 8D 05 D4        STA $D405
C01A 8D 06 D4        STA $D406
C01D 58              CLI
C01E 60              RTS
C01F A5 C5           LDA $C5
C021 A2 00           LDX #$00
C023 A0 00           LDY #$00
C025 DD 43 C0        CMP $C043,X
C028 F0 0A           BEQ $C034
C02A E8              INX
C02B C8              INY
C02C C8              INY
C02D E0 0F           CPX #$0F
C02F D0 F4           BNE $C025
C031 4C 31 EA        JMP $EA31
C034 B9 51 C0        LDA $C051,Y
C037 8D 01 D4        STA $D401
C03A B9 52 C0        LDA $C052,Y
C03D 8D 00 D4        STA $D400
C040 4C 31 EA        JMP $EA31
```

```
.:C043 3E 09 0E 11 16 19 1E 21
.:C04B 26 29 2E 31 36 3C 11 25
.:C053 13 3F 15 9A 16 E3 19 B1
.:C05B 1C D6 20 5E 22 4B 26 7E
.:C063 2B 34 2D C6 33 61 39 AC
.:C06B 00 00 A8 68 AA 68 4C 31
```

Sometimes you will want text, listings, etc, to be only in specified columns. The following program sets the screen to 40 columns but can be adjusted to provide from one to 128 columns by POKEing location 881 with *twice* the number of columns that you want it to list in. All the BASIC listings in this book were listed using this utility, with a 40 column listing width (881 containing 80). The program works by intercepting the character output vector at $0326 and $0327. What the program does is check if the computer is at the value in 881 *2 and if it is, then print a carriage return. It then jumps to the normal routine to finish.

```
033C AD 26 03      LDA $0326
033F 8D 72 03      STA $0372
0342 AD 27 03      LDA $0327
0345 8D 73 03      STA $0373
0348 A9 53         LDA #$53
034A 8D 26 03      STA $0326
034D A9 03         LDA #$03
034F 8D 27 03      STA $0327
0352 60            RTS
0353 C9 0D         CMP #$0D
0355 F0 0B         BEQ $0362
0357 CE 74 03      DEC $0374
035A CE 74 03      DEC $0374
035D D0 0B         BNE $036A
035F 20 6E 03      JSR $036E
0362 AD 71 03      LDA $0371
0365 8D 74 03      STA $0374
0368 A9 0D         LDA #$0D
036A 20 6E 03      JSR $036E
036D 60            RTS
036E 6C 72 03      JMP ($0372)
0371 50 CA         BVC $033D
```

RASTER SCAN GRAPHICS

The raster beam is the beam of light in a TV or monitor that creates the picture. It moves down the screen one line at a time until it reaches the bottom. It then goes back to the top and starts again. This series of operations happens 60 times a second.

A computer sends a signal into the TV or monitor which is used to create the picture that you see. The Commodore 64 is one of the few computers that can control the raster beam directly, stopping and starting it at will. This allows us to do things that would normally be impossible. For example we could have three different screen colours (location 53281) on the screen at once, make the screen half text and half high resolution, put more than eight sprites on the screen at once, and much, much more. The reason that this is possible is that we are able to interrupt the raster beam before it has finished the frame and change certain things. This causes no, or very little, flicker.

The first thing that must be done to set up a raster is to first set up an IRQ interrupt to the start of our routine. The first line of the interrupt must be as follows:

```
LDA $D019
```

Location $D019 (53273) is the interrupt flag register and tells us whether an interrupt has occurred or not. This can be seen by looking at bit zero of this register. Therefore, the next lines of the program perform an AND #$01 on the value in A (from 53273).

```
STA $D019
AND #$01
BNE main raster program
JMP $EA31
main raster program . . .
```

The reason that the second line is STA $D019 is that if a raster interrupt has occurred, we want to turn it off. This is done by putting a '1' into the raster bit (bit zero). This resets the register so that another interrupt can occur when we have finished our routine. This may seem strange—turning the bit on when we really want to turn it off—however, to turn the bit off we must put a '1' into it. This makes the bit contain zero. Don't ask me why, but that is how the video chip works!

The next line (BNE main. . .) checks if the value in A is not zero, i.e. an interrupt bit has been set. If it has, it branches to the rest of our program. If there is no bit set, it jumps to the normal IRQ routine.

```
LDA #$01
STA $D01A
CLI
RTS
```

The start of the program sets up an IRQ interrupt. Then we store the value of the first interrupt into $D012 (53266)—location $D011 is then ANDed with $7F. What this does is reset the ninth bit of the raster so that the interrupt occurs at the line we have specified. If we do this, the raster interrupt will not work. Finally, we must turn the raster interrupt on—this is done by setting bit zero of location $D01A to '1'.

Back to the interrupt itself, we must now check the value of the raster in location 53266 to see if it is our first or second interrupt (in this example). The following lines achieve this:

LDA $D012

BMI $ other raster   : Is the raster greater than 128? If yes, then GOTO the routine that resets us to the first raster.

Now we must change the raster to the next raster position and do the work that we require. The following lines are those remaining needed to make up a raster to colour the screen in two different colours.

Next we need to find out where the raster beam is. This is because we must make at least two interrupts per frame: one to reset us to the beginning and the others to do the changes that we require. The location that we read is location 53266, and this location when read tells us the current line that the raster beam is on. (It is the low eight bits of the position—the ninth bit is bit seven of location 53265—but we only need to use location 53266 for raster work.) When we write to it, it sets an internal flag that makes the raster be interrupted at the line that we wrote into location 53266.

Here is the routine that we use to set up a raster interrupt:

```
SEI
LDA #$ lobyte of start
STA $0314
LDA #$ hibyte of start
STA $0315
LDA #$ first raster interrupt at line
STA $D012
LDA $D011
AND #$7F
STA $D011
LDA $D012
BMI $other
LDA #$7F
STA $D012
LDA #$00
STA $D020
STA $D021
JMP $FEBC
other LDA #$FF
STA $D012
LDA #$02
STA $D020
STA $D021
JMP $FEBC
```

The JMP $FEBC is the routine normally used to end a raster interrupt. This just tidies things up for us and ends the interrupt.

86

Here is the completed raster program that we have gradually created above. You will notice that there is some flicker, especially if you press a key. There is a better way of creating a raster which we will see later.

```
.
2000 78              SEI
2001 A9 1F           LDA #$1F
2003 8D 14 03        STA $0314
2006 A9 20           LDA #$20
2008 8D 15 03        STA $0315
200B 58              CLI
200C A9 64           LDA #$64
200E 8D 12 D0        STA $D012
2011 AD 11 D0        LDA $D011
2014 29 7F           AND #$7F
2016 8D 11 D0        STA $D011
2019 A9 01           LDA #$01
201B 8D 1A D0        STA $D01A
201E 60              RTS
201F AD 19 D0        LDA $D019
2022 29 01           AND #$01
2024 D0 03           BNE $2029
2026 4C 31 EA        JMP $EA31
2029 8D 19 D0        STA $D019
202C AD 12 D0        LDA $D012
202F F0 10           BEQ $2041
2031 A9 00           LDA #$00
2033 8D 12 D0        STA $D012
2036 A9 00           LDA #$00
2038 8D 20 D0        STA $D020
203B 8D 21 D0        STA $D021
203E 4C BC FE        JMP $FEBC
2041 A9 64           LDA #$64
2043 8D 12 D0        STA $D012
2046 A9 02           LDA #$02
2048 8D 20 D0        STA $D020
204B 8D 21 D0        STA $D021
204E 4C BC FE        JMP $FEBC
```

Here is a raster program that puts a text and high resolution graphics on the screen at once. To start it, type SYS 4096. You will notice that there is some flicker—this is a result of the way that this interrupt has been achieved.

```
1000 78              SEI
1001 A9 1F           LDA #$1F
1003 A2 10           LDX #$10
1005 8D 14 03        STA $0314
1008 8E 15 03        STX $0315
100B 58              CLI
100C A9 01           LDA #$01
100E 8D 12 D0        STA $D012
1011 AD 11 D0        LDA $D011
1014 29 7F           AND #$7F
1016 8D 11 D0        STA $D011
1019 A9 01           LDA #$01
101B 8D 1A D0        STA $D01A
101E 60              RTS
101F AD 19 D0        LDA $D019
1022 29 01           AND #$01
1024 D0 03           BNE $1029
1026 4C 31 EA        JMP $EA31
1029 8D 19 D0        STA $D019
102C AD 12 D0        LDA $D012
102F 30 17           BMI $1048
1031 A9 96           LDA #$96
1033 8D 12 D0        STA $D012
1036 A9 47           LDA #$47
1038 8D 00 DD        STA $DD00
103B A9 15           LDA #$15
103D 8D 18 D0        STA $D018
1040 A9 1B           LDA #$1B
1042 8D 11 D0        STA $D011
1045 4C BC FE        JMP $FEBC
1048 A9 08           LDA #$08
104A 8D 18 D0        STA $D018
104D A9 01           LDA #$01
104F 8D 12 D0        STA $D012
1052 AD 00 DD        LDA $DD00
```

```
1055 29 FE          AND #$FE
1057 8D 00 DD        STA $DD00
105A AD 11 D0        LDA $D011
105D 09 20           ORA #$20
105F 8D 11 D0        STA $D011
1062 4C BC FE        JMP $FEBC
.
```

Now we will see how to improve the raster routine so that there is no flicker. The secret to this involves two factors:

1: Set bit seven of location 56333 to zero. This has the effect of stopping the computer from performing a normal IRQ (disabling the IRQ). Instead, only our raster interrupt will occur. The computer would not normally function if we did this but our new routine takes care of that problem. (As the normal IRQ is disabled, there is no conflict between raster interrupts and IRQ interrupts.) The raster calls the IRQ every three interrupts, thus removing any flicker.

2: Only jump to $EA31 at every third raster interrupt. This means that our routine must take over for the other two interrupts and pull the register contents off the stack, and then return from the interrupt with RTI. This is required or you'll find that the stack will fill up and the computer will probably crash. This is because the computer puts the values of the registers onto the stack at each interrupt. (If we called the IRQ every raster interrupt we would slow the computer down quite a lot.)

Here is a program that puts text, high resolution and multi-colour high resolution graphics on the screen at the same time using the above method.

```
4000 78             SEI
4001 A9 7F          LDA #$7F
4003 8D 0D DC       STA $DC0D
4006 A9 01          LDA #$01
4008 8D 1A D0       STA $D01A
400B A9 03          LDA #$03
400D 85 FB          STA $FB
```

89

```
400F AD 70 40      LDA $4070
4012 8D 12 D0      STA $D012
4015 A9 18         LDA #$18
4017 8D 11 D0      STA $D011
401A AD 14 03      LDA $0314
401D 8D 6E 40      STA $406E
4020 AD 15 03      LDA $0315
4023 8D 6F 40      STA $406F
4026 A9 32         LDA #$32
4028 8D 14 03      STA $0314
402B A9 40         LDA #$40
402D 8D 15 03      STA $0315
4030 58            CLI
4031 60            RTS
4032 AD 19 D0      LDA $D019
4035 8D 19 D0      STA $D019
4038 29 01         AND #$01
403A F0 2B         BEQ $4067
403C C6 FB         DEC $FB
403E 10 04         BPL $4044
4040 A9 02         LDA #$02
4042 85 FB         STA $FB
4044 A6 FB         LDX $FB
4046 BD 73 40      LDA $4073,X
4049 8D 21 D0      STA $D021
404C BD 76 40      LDA $4076,X
404F 8D 11 D0      STA $D011
4052 BD 79 40      LDA $4079,X
4055 8D 16 D0      STA $D016
4058 BD 7C 40      LDA $407C,X
405B 8D 18 D0      STA $D018
405E BD 70 40      LDA $4070,X
4061 8D 12 D0      STA $D012
4064 8A            TXA
4065 F0 06         BEQ $406D
4067 68            PLA
4068 A8            TAY
4069 68            PLA
406A AA            TAX
406B 68            PLA
```

```
406C 40              RTI
406D 4C 31 EA        JMP $EA31

.
.:4070 31 AA 81 00 06 00 3B 1B
.:4078 3B 18 08 08 18 14 18 00
.:4080 FF FF BF 90 50 C8 C8 98
```

Enter the raster interrupt and start it with G **4000** or SYS 16384.

Now type in the following BASIC program. This will demonstrate this raster program:

```
10 PRINT"{CLR}":FORA=1TO10:PRINT:NEXT:PRINT"
THIS IS TEXT !!!"
60 FORA=1024TO1383:POKEA,114:NEXT:FORA=1
384TO1423:POKEA,6:NEXT
70 FORA=1664TO2023:POKEA,234:NEXT
80 FORA=55936TO56295:POKEA,13:NEXT
90 FORA=8192TO11391:POKEA,0:POKEA+4800,0
:NEXT
100 B=8192
110 H=40:C=0:FORX=0TO319:GOSUB150:NEXT
120 H=160:C=0:FORX=0TO319STEP2:GOSUB150:
NEXT:C=40:FORX=1TO319STEP2:GOSUB150:NEXT

130 C=80:FORX=0TO319STEP2:W=0:GOSUB150:W
=1:GOSUB150:NEXT
140 GOTO140
150 Y=INT(H+20*SIN(X/10+C)):CH=INT(X/8):
RO=INT(Y/8):LN=YAND7
160 BY=B+RO*320+8*CH+LN:BI=ABS(7-(XAND7)
-W)
170 POKEBY,PEEK(BY)OR(2^BI):RETURN
```

Finally, here is a program that does the 'impossible'. It puts three different border colours, three screen colours, normal text, multi-colour text, extended colour text and 24 sprites on the screen at the same time!!!

91

The top of the screen is blue, the border is blue and is in multi-colour character mode. The middle of the screen is yellow, the border is yellow and contains normal text. The bottom of the screen is red, the border is red and is in extended colour mode. (Each of the sections have eight sprites in each.)

To start the program, type SYS 16384 and then SYS 16546. To see the sprites, use the following lines:

FOR A=2040 TO 2047:POKE A,13:NEXT
FOR A=832 TO 832+62:POKE A,255:NEXT

The sprites in the program are all controlled by the same sprite data register (2040–2047) and therefore the three leftmost sprites are the same. The program could easily be changed to allow 24 different sprites on the screen at once by adding another LDA ....., X and a STA 2040,X to change the position that the sprite gets its data from. To see the fact that the program actually puts three 'clones' of each sprite, try the following line:

FOR A=0 TO 255:POKE 53248, A:NEXT

Enjoy yourself with the raster graphics. They are hard to understand at first but they are worth it once you do!!

```
.
4000 78          SEI
4001 A9 7F       LDA #$7F
4003 8D 0D DC    STA $DC0D
4006 A9 01       LDA #$01
4008 8D 1A D0    STA $D01A
400B A9 03       LDA #$03
400D 85 FB       STA $FB
400F AD 76 40    LDA $4076
4012 8D 12 D0    STA $D012
4015 A9 18       LDA #$18
4017 8D 11 D0    STA $D011
```

```
401A AD 14 03    LDA $0314
401D 8D 74 40    STA $4074
4020 AD 15 03    LDA $0315
4023 8D 75 40    STA $4075
4026 A9 32       LDA #$32
4028 8D 14 03    STA $0314
402B A9 40       LDA #$40
402D 8D 15 03    STA $0315
4030 58          CLI
4031 60          RTS
4032 AD 19 D0    LDA $D019
4035 8D 19 D0    STA $D019
4038 29 01       AND #$01
403A F0 31       BEQ $406D
403C C6 FB       DEC $FB
403E 10 04       BPL $4044
4040 A9 02       LDA #$02
4042 85 FB       STA $FB
4044 A6 FB       LDX $FB
4046 BD 79 40    LDA $4079,X
4049 8D 21 D0    STA $D021
404C BD 7C 40    LDA $407C,X
404F 8D 11 D0    STA $D011
4052 BD 7F 40    LDA $407F,X
4055 8D 20 D0    STA $D020
4058 BD 85 40    LDA $4085,X
405B 8D 16 D0    STA $D016
405E BD 82 40    LDA $4082,X
4061 20 89 40    JSR $4089
4064 BD 76 40    LDA $4076,X
4067 8D 12 D0    STA $D012
406A 8A          TXA
406B F0 06       BEQ $4073
406D 68          PLA
406E A8          TAY
406F 68          PLA
4070 AA          TAX
4071 68          PLA
4072 40          RTI
4073 4C 31 EA    JMP $EA31
```

```
.
.:4076 31 AF 81 02 07 06 5B 1B
.:407E 1B 02 07 06 BF 90 50 C8
.:4086 C8 98 C8 8D 01 D0 8D 03
.
.
.
4089 8D 01 D0        STA $D001
408C 8D 03 D0        STA $D003
408F 8D 05 D0        STA $D005
4092 8D 07 D0        STA $D007
4095 8D 09 D0        STA $D009
4098 8D 0B D0        STA $D00B
409B 8D 0D D0        STA $D00D
409E 8D 0F D0        STA $D00F
40A1 60              RTS
40A2 A9 FF           LDA #$FF
40A4 8D 15 D0        STA $D015
40A7 A2 00           LDX #$00
40A9 A0 00           LDY #$00
40AB A9 32           LDA #$32
40AD 9D 00 D0        STA $D000,X
40B0 E8              INX
40B1 E8              INX
40B2 69 19           ADC #$19
40B4 E0 10           CPX #$10
40B6 D0 F5           BNE $40AD
40B8 A2 00           LDX #$00
40BA A9 08           LDA #$08
40BC 9D 27 D0        STA $D027,X
40BF 18              CLC
40C0 69 01           ADC #$01
40C2 E8              INX
40C3 E0 08           CPX #$08
40C5 D0 F5           BNE $40BC
40C7 60              RTS
.
```

HIGH RESOLUTION GRAPHICS

The Commodore 64 has probably the best graphics of any home microcomputer around at this moment in time. However, there are no commands in the ROM to utilise this capability. You could write graphic routines in BASIC but they are so slow that it would be barely worthwhile. Contained in the pages to come is a graphics toolkit complete with the following utilities—all in machine code.

Graph : Turns on the high resolution screen.
Nrm   : Turns off the high resolution screen.
Colour : Sets the screen colour, border colour, text colour and multi-colour colours 1, 2 and 3.
Clg   : Clears and colours the high resolution screen.
Fill   : Fills areas of memory with a byte, eg. the colour of the high resolution screen.
Invert : Inverts an area on the high resolution screen or memory, changes the byte 00010000 to 11101111.
Plot   : Plots a point on the high resolution screen.
Unplot : Removes a point from the high resolution screen.
Char : Puts an eight by eight character on the screen (or your own programmed characters).

Just to give you an example of the speed of these routines, the CLG routine in BASIC would take 1 minute 22.71 seconds—yet in machine code CLG takes just 0.133 seconds. That's an improvement of 640 times!

All the commands presented here are accessed as 'SYS' commands, but in the next part of the book it will be explained how they can be called from BASIC keywords.

Before we start I'd better explain how these commands are able to take off variables from the BASIC text. This is done using ROM routines (as was explained in the *ROM disassembly* section) but to reiterate, they are as follows:

Routine

$AEFD   : Checks if the next character in BASIC text is a comma—if not it prints 'SYNTAX ERROR' message and returns to BASIC.

$AD8A   : Evaluates an expression in BASIC text and puts it in FAC.

$B7F7   : Converts the value in FAC into an integer in the range zero to 65535 and puts the result in $14 (lo-byte) and $15 (hi-byte) and return to BASIC.

Firstly, let's take a look at the command 'graph'. What this command does is switch on the high resolution screen which is located at 24576 ($6000) and turn on the colour screen which is located at 16384. The command stands on its own to turn on the high resolution screen, type SYS 49152. (You can also make the SYS calls variables, ie. GRAPH = 49152 and then type SYS GRAPH.)

```
.
CØØØ A9 16        LDA #$16
CØØ2 8D ØØ DD     STA $DDØØ
CØØ5 A9 Ø8        LDA #$Ø8
CØØ7 8D 18 DØ     STA $DØ18
CØØA AD 11 DØ     LDA $DØ11
CØØD Ø9 2Ø        ORA #$2Ø
CØØF 8D 11 DØ     STA $DØ11
CØ12 6Ø           RTS
```

Now here is the complementary command to 'graph'. . . 'NRM'. This turns the high resolution screen off and goes back to the text screen, which is untouched by any high resolution commands or operations in these routines (unlike others). To use this command, type SYS 49171 or NRM = 49171 : SYS NRM.

```
CØ13 A9 15        LDA #$15
CØ15 8D 18 DØ     STA $DØ18
CØ18 A9 1B        LDA #$1B
```

96

```
CØ1A 8D 11 DØ        STA $DØ11
CØ1D A9 17           LDA #$17
CØ1F 8D ØØ DD        STA $DDØØ
CØ22 6Ø              RTS
```

Now we need to clear the screen for use and the following routine does just that. It fills the high resolution screen with zeros and fills them with the colour specified in the command 'colour'. The syntax for the command is SYS 49187, colour, colour or CLG = 49187: SYS CLG, colour, colour. The two 'colour' instructions after the command are respectively the foreground (dot) and the background colours. This is for 320 by 200 resolution graphics.

The command works using Indexed Indirect mode (STA ($FB),Y) to fill the 8000 bytes of the high resolution screen with zeros and the colour between 16384 and 17383. The colour control is as follows. . .

The high nibble (four bits) is the foreground colour and the low nibble is the background colours in binary, eg. to get blue lines (foreground) and a yellow background:

0111   0110

7   6
yellow   blue

So, from the above example it can be seen that the byte is binary 01110110 which is 118 in decimal. The program calculates this and POKES the values into the colour memory.

```
CØ23 2Ø FD AE        JSR $AEFD
CØ26 2Ø 8A AD        JSR $AD8A
CØ29 2Ø F7 B7        JSR $B7F7
CØ2C A5 15           LDA $15
CØ2E FØ Ø3           BEQ $CØ33
CØ3Ø 4C 48 B2        JMP $B248
CØ33 A5 14           LDA $14
CØ35 8D 82 CØ        STA $CØ82
CØ38 2Ø FD AE        JSR $AEFD
```

97

```
C03B 20 8A AD     JSR $AD8A
C03E 20 F7 B7     JSR $B7F7
C041 A5 15        LDA $15
C043 F0 03        BEQ $C048
C045 4C 48 B2     JMP $B248
C048 A5 14        LDA $14
C04A 0A           ASL
C04B 0A           ASL
C04C 0A           ASL
C04D 0A           ASL
C04E 0D 82 C0     ORA $C082
C051 8D 82 C0     STA $C082
C054 A9 00        LDA #$00
C056 85 FB        STA $FB
C058 A9 60        LDA #$60
C05A 85 FC        STA $FC
C05C A0 00        LDY #$00
C05E A9 00        LDA #$00
C060 91 FB        STA ($FB),Y
C062 C8           INY
C063 D0 FB        BNE $C060
C065 E6 FC        INC $FC
C067 A6 FC        LDX $FC
C069 E0 80        CPX #$80
C06B D0 F3        BNE $C060
C06D AD 82 C0     LDA $C082
C070 A2 00        LDX #$00
C072 9D 00 40     STA $4000,X
C075 9D 00 41     STA $4100,X
C078 9D 00 42     STA $4200,X
C07B 9D 00 43     STA $4300,X
C07E E8           INX
C07F D0 F1        BNE $C072
C081 60           RTS
C082 00           BRK
```

Now, POKEing to achieve colour is a tedious operation.
Here is a routine that changes this—it allows you to enter
one command to change the border, screen, text and
multicolour 1, 2 and 3 colours. The syntax is SYS colour,

screen, border, text, multi1, multi2, multi3 (where 'colour' = 49379).

```
CØE3 20 FD AE      JSR $AEFD
CØE6 20 26 C1      JSR $C126
CØE9 A5 14         LDA $14
CØEB 8D 21 DØ      STA $DØ21
CØEE 20 FD AE      JSR $AEFD
CØF1 20 26 C1      JSR $C126
CØF4 A5 14         LDA $14
CØF6 8D 20 DØ      STA $DØ20
CØF9 20 FD AE      JSR $AEFD
CØFC 20 26 C1      JSR $C126
CØFF A5 14         LDA $14
C101 8D 86 Ø2      STA $Ø286
C104 20 FD AE      JSR $AEFD
C107 20 26 C1      JSR $C126
C10A A5 14         LDA $14
C10C 8D 22 DØ      STA $DØ22
C10F 20 FD AE      JSR $AEFD
C112 20 26 C1      JSR $C126
C115 A5 14         LDA $14
C117 8D 23 DØ      STA $DØ23
C11A 20 FD AE      JSR $AEFD
C11D 20 26 C1      JSR $C126
C120 A5 14         LDA $14
C122 8D 24 DØ      STA $DØ24
C125 60            RTS
C126 20 8A AD      JSR $AD8A
C129 20 F7 B7      JSR $B7F7
C12C A5 15         LDA $15
C12E DØ Ø1         BNE $C131
C130 60            RTS
C131 4C 48 B2      JMP $B248
```

You might want to fill an area of the high resolution screen or memory with a byte, eg. to fill the memory with NOP commands or fill the high resolution screen with 255 (fill it in completely). Well, here is a command that does this and the syntax is SYS fill, start, finish, byte (where 'fill' = 49283).

```
C083  20 FD AE      JSR $AEFD
C086  20 8A AD      JSR $AD8A
C089  20 F7 B7      JSR $B7F7
C08C  A5 14         LDA $14
C08E  85 FB         STA $FB
C090  A5 15         LDA $15
C092  85 FC         STA $FC
C094  20 FD AE      JSR $AEFD
C097  20 8A AD      JSR $AD8A
C09A  20 F7 B7      JSR $B7F7
C09D  A5 14         LDA $14
C09F  8D 3C 03      STA $033C
C0A2  A5 15         LDA $15
C0A4  8D 3D 03      STA $033D
C0A7  20 FD AE      JSR $AEFD
C0AA  20 8A AD      JSR $AD8A
C0AD  20 F7 B7      JSR $B7F7
C0B0  A5 15         LDA $15
C0B2  F0 03         BEQ $C0B7
C0B4  4C 48 B2      JMP $B248
C0B7  A5 14         LDA $14
C0B9  8D 3E 03      STA $033E
C0BC  A0 00         LDY #$00
C0BE  AD 3E 03      LDA $033E
C0C1  91 FB         STA ($FB),Y
C0C3  20 DA C0      JSR $C0DA
C0C6  A5 FB         LDA $FB
C0C8  CD 3C 03      CMP $033C
C0CB  F0 03         BEQ $C0D0
C0CD  4C BC C0      JMP $C0BC
C0D0  A5 FC         LDA $FC
C0D2  CD 3D 03      CMP $033D
C0D5  F0 0B         BEQ $C0E2
C0D7  4C BC C0      JMP $C0BC
C0DA  E6 FB         INC $FB
C0DC  F0 01         BEQ $C0DF
C0DE  60            RTS
C0DF  E6 FC         INC $FC
C0E1  60            RTS
C0E2  60            RTS
```

Say you don't want to fill an area with a byte but you want to invert them for security reasons, or you want to invert a picture turning every dot that is on to off and *vice versa*. Here is just such a routine and the syntax is SYN invert, start, finish (where 'invert' = 49920).

```
C300  20 FD AE    JSR $AEFD
C303  20 8A AD    JSR $AD8A
C306  20 F7 B7    JSR $B7F7
C309  A5 14       LDA $14
C30B  85 FB       STA $FB
C30D  A5 15       LDA $15
C30F  85 FC       STA $FC
C311  20 FD AE    JSR $AEFD
C314  20 8A AD    JSR $AD8A
C317  20 F7 B7    JSR $B7F7
C31A  A5 14       LDA $14
C31C  8D 3C 03    STA $033C
C31F  A5 15       LDA $15
C321  8D 3D 03    STA $033D
C324  A0 00       LDY #$00
C326  A9 FF       LDA #$FF
C328  51 FB       EOR ($FB),Y
C32A  91 FB       STA ($FB),Y
C32C  20 43 C3    JSR $C343
C32F  A5 FB       LDA $FB
C331  CD 3C 03    CMP $033C
C334  F0 03       BEQ $C339
C336  4C 24 C3    JMP $C324
C339  A5 FC       LDA $FC
C33B  CD 3D 03    CMP $033D
C33E  F0 0B       BEQ $C34B
C340  4C 24 C3    JMP $C324
C343  E6 FB       INC $FB
C345  F0 01       BEQ $C348
C347  60          RTS
C348  E6 FC       INC $FC
C34A  60          RTS
C34B  60          RTS
```

Now none of this is of any use if we cannot plot points on the screen—the following routine will come in very useful. The reason that the routine is fast is that it doesn't use a lot of loops to calculate the screen byte to POKE and the bit to set. It does not loop at all, in fact; it uses tables of bytes to do this and calculates the bit to turn on or off. This is what the monitor after the disassembly is. The syntax of the command is SYS plot,x,y (where 'x' is the X co-ordinate between zero and 319, 'y' is the Y co-ordinate between zero and 199 and 'plot' = 49464).

```
C134 A9 FF          LDA #$FF
C136 D0 02          BNE $C13A
C138 A9 00          LDA #$00
C13A 8D E8 C1       STA $C1E8
C13D 20 FD AE       JSR $AEFD
C140 20 EB B7       JSR $B7EB
C143 E0 C8          CPX #$C8
C145 B0 5E          BCS $C1A5
C147 A5 14          LDA $14
C149 C9 40          CMP #$40
C14B A5 15          LDA $15
C14D E9 01          SBC #$01
C14F B0 54          BCS $C1A5
C151 8A             TXA
C152 4A             LSR
C153 4A             LSR
C154 4A             LSR
C155 0A             ASL
C156 A8             TAY
C157 B9 A6 C1       LDA $C1A6,Y
C15A 85 FD          STA $FD
C15C B9 A7 C1       LDA $C1A7,Y
C15F 85 FE          STA $FE
C161 8A             TXA
C162 29 07          AND #$07
C164 18             CLC
C165 65 FD          ADC $FD
C167 85 FD          STA $FD
C169 A5 FE          LDA $FE
```

```
C16B 69 00        ADC #$00
C16D 85 FE        STA $FE
C16F A5 14        LDA $14
C171 29 07        AND #$07
C173 A8           TAY
C174 A5 14        LDA $14
C176 29 F8        AND #$F8
C178 18           CLC
C179 65 FD        ADC $FD
C17B 85 FD        STA $FD
C17D A5 FE        LDA $FE
C17F 65 15        ADC $15
C181 85 FE        STA $FE
C183 A5 FD        LDA $FD
C185 18           CLC
C186 69 00        ADC #$00
C188 85 FD        STA $FD
C18A A5 FE        LDA $FE
C18C 69 60        ADC #$60
C18E 85 FE        STA $FE
C190 A2 00        LDX #$00
C192 A1 FD        LDA ($FD,X)
C194 2C E8 C1     BIT $C1E8
C197 10 06        BPL $C19F
C199 39 E0 C1     AND $C1E0,Y
C19C 4C A2 C1     JMP $C1A2
C19F 19 D8 C1     ORA $C1D8,Y
C1A2 81 FD        STA ($FD,X)
C1A4 60           RTS
C1A5 60           RTS
.
.:C1A6 00 00 40 01 80 02 C0 03
.:C1AE 00 05 40 06 80 07 C0 08
.:C1B6 00 0A 40 0B 80 0C C0 0D
.:C1BE 00 0F 40 10 80 11 C0 12
.:C1C6 00 14 40 15 80 16 C0 17
.:C1CE 00 19 40 1A 80 1B C0 1C
.:C1D6 00 1E 80 40 20 10 08 04
.:C1DE 02 01 7F BF DF EF F7 FB
.:C1E6 FD FE 00 4C 48 B2 20 FD
```

There is a complementary command to 'plot'. It is 'unplot' and it has the syntax SYS unplot,x,y (where unplot = 49460, and 'x' and 'y' are the X and Y co-ordinates of the point to be UNPLOTted (deleted)). It uses the same routine as the command detailed above but with a different entry point.

Finally, we come to the last program relevant to high resolution graphics. It is 'char' and allows you to put any text character onto the high resolution screen. It works in the same format as the text screen, ie. 40 columns by 25 rows. The syntax is SYS char,x,y, character (where 'character' is the POKE code of the character from zero to 255, 'x' is the X co-ordinate of the position from zero to 39 and 'y' is the Y co-ordinate of the position from zero to 24 and char = 49644). Variables can be used in place of any number in any of the above examples. If the value exceeds the allowed amounts, then an 'ILLEGAL QUANTITY' error will occur.

```
C1E9 4C 48 B2      JMP $B248
C1EC 20 FD AE      JSR $AEFD
C1EF 20 CB C2      JSR $C2CB
C1F2 A5 14         LDA $14
C1F4 C9 28         CMP #$28
C1F6 B0 F1         BCS $C1E9
C1F8 8D F9 C2      STA $C2F9
C1FB 20 FD AE      JSR $AEFD
C1FE 20 CB C2      JSR $C2CB
C201 A5 14         LDA $14
C203 C9 19         CMP #$19
C205 B0 E2         BCS $C1E9
C207 8D FA C2      STA $C2FA
C20A AD F9 C2      LDA $C2F9
C20D 8D F6 C2      STA $C2F6
C210 A9 08         LDA #$08
C212 8D F7 C2      STA $C2F7
C215 20 D9 C2      JSR $C2D9
C218 AD F4 C2      LDA $C2F4
C21B 85 FB         STA $FB
C21D AD F5 C2      LDA $C2F5
C220 85 FC         STA $FC
```

```
C222 AD FA C2    LDA $C2FA
C225 8D F6 C2    STA $C2F6
C228 A9 28       LDA #$28
C22A 8D F7 C2    STA $C2F7
C22D 20 D9 C2    JSR $C2D9
C230 AD F4 C2    LDA $C2F4
C233 8D FE C2    STA $C2FE
C236 AD F5 C2    LDA $C2F5
C239 8D FF C2    STA $C2FF
C23C A2 07       LDX #$07
C23E AD F4 C2    LDA $C2F4
C241 6D FE C2    ADC $C2FE
C244 8D F4 C2    STA $C2F4
C247 AD F5 C2    LDA $C2F5
C24A 69 00       ADC #$00
C24C 8D F5 C2    STA $C2F5
C24F CA          DEX
C250 D0 EC       BNE $C23E
C252 A2 07       LDX #$07
C254 AD F5 C2    LDA $C2F5
C257 18          CLC
C258 6D FF C2    ADC $C2FF
C25B 8D F5 C2    STA $C2F5
C25E CA          DEX
C25F D0 F3       BNE $C254
C261 AD F5 C2    LDA $C2F5
C264 18          CLC
C265 69 60       ADC #$60
C267 8D F5 C2    STA $C2F5
C26A A5 FB       LDA $FB
C26C 18          CLC
C26D 6D F4 C2    ADC $C2F4
C270 85 FB       STA $FB
C272 A5 FC       LDA $FC
C274 6D F5 C2    ADC $C2F5
C277 85 FC       STA $FC
C279 20 FD AE    JSR $AEFD
C27C 20 CB C2    JSR $C2CB
C27F A5 14       LDA $14
C281 8D FC C2    STA $C2FC
```

```
C284 AD FC C2      LDA $C2FC
C287 8D F6 C2      STA $C2F6
C28A A9 08         LDA #$08
C28C 8D F7 C2      STA $C2F7
C28F 20 D9 C2      JSR $C2D9
C292 AD F4 C2      LDA $C2F4
C295 85 FD         STA $FD
C297 AD F5 C2      LDA $C2F5
C29A 18            CLC
C29B 69 D0         ADC #$D0
C29D 85 FE         STA $FE
C29F A9 00         LDA #$00
C2A1 8D F8 C2      STA $C2F8
C2A4 78            SEI
C2A5 A9 33         LDA #$33
C2A7 85 01         STA $01
C2A9 A0 00         LDY #$00
C2AB B1 FD         LDA ($FD),Y
C2AD 91 FB         STA ($FB),Y
C2AF E6 FB         INC $FB
C2B1 D0 02         BNE $C2B5
C2B3 E6 FC         INC $FC
C2B5 E6 FD         INC $FD
C2B7 D0 02         BNE $C2BB
C2B9 E6 FE         INC $FE
C2BB EE F8 C2      INC $C2F8
C2BE AD F8 C2      LDA $C2F8
C2C1 C9 08         CMP #$08
C2C3 D0 E6         BNE $C2AB
C2C5 A9 37         LDA #$37
C2C7 85 01         STA $01
C2C9 58            CLI
C2CA 60            RTS
C2CB 20 8A AD      JSR $AD8A
C2CE 20 F7 B7      JSR $B7F7
C2D1 A5 15         LDA $15
C2D3 F0 03         BEQ $C2D8
C2D5 4C 48 B2      JMP $B248
C2D8 60            RTS
C2D9 A9 00         LDA #$00
```

106

```
C2DB 8D F4 C2      STA $C2F4
C2DE A2 08         LDX #$08
C2E0 4E F6 C2      LSR $C2F6
C2E3 90 04         BCC $C2E9
C2E5 18            CLC
C2E6 6D F7 C2      ADC $C2F7
C2E9 6A            ROR
C2EA 6E F4 C2      ROR $C2F4
C2ED CA            DEX
C2EE D0 F0         BNE $C2E0
C2F0 8D F5 C2      STA $C2F5
C2F3 60            RTS
C2F4 00            BRK
C2F5 00            BRK
C2F6 00            BRK
C2F7 00            BRK
C2F8 00            BRK
C2F9 00            BRK
C2FA 00            BRK
C2FB 00            BRK
C2FC 00            BRK
C2FD 00            BRK
C2FE 00            BRK
C2FF 00            BRK
```

Here is a BASIC program that demonstrates the use of the above commands:

```
0 GRAPH=49152:NRM=49152+19:CLG=49152+35
10 FILL=49283:COLOUR=49379:PLOT=49464
20 UNPLOT=49460:CHAR=49644:INVERT=49920
30 SYSCOLOUR,0,0,7,1,2,3
40 SYSGRAPH
50 SYSCLG,0,7
55 PRINT"{CLR}HIRES GRAPHICS !!! - CIRCLES"
60 FORA=0TO39
70 SYSCHAR,A,10,PEEK(1024+A)
80 NEXT
90 C=110:D=100
100 FORA=0TO6.5STEP0.01
```

```
110 X=C*SIN(A)+160:Y=D*COS(A)+100
120 SYS PLOT,X,Y
130 NEXT
140 Y=0:FORX=0TO319STEP2
150 SYSPLOT,X,Y:SYSPLOT,X+1,Y
160 SYSPLOT,319-X,Y:SYSPLOT,319-X-1,Y
170 Y=Y+1:NEXT
180 FORA=0TO319
190 SYSPLOT,A,0
200 SYSPLOT,A,199
210 NEXT
220 FORA=0TO199
230 SYSPLOT,0,A
240 SYSPLOT,319,199-A
250 NEXT
260 SYSINVERT,24576,32768
270 FORR=0TO500:NEXT
280 SYSINVERT,24576,32768
290 FORA=0TO255
300 SYSFILL,16384,17383,A
310 NEXT
320 FORR=0TO500:NEXT
330 RUN
```

ADDING COMMANDS TO BASIC

There are many ways of adding commands to BASIC, but the method that I am going to use here is moving BASIC into RAM and altering it to suit our purposes. This section will explain how to add the following new commands to the BASIC language:

GRAPH : Turns on the high resolution screen.
NRM : Turns off high resolution screen.
CLG : Clears the high resolution screen.
FILL : Fills areas of memory with a byte.
CHAR : Puts a character on the high resolution screen.
COLOUR : Changes the border, screen, text and multi1,2,3.
PLOT : Plots a point on the high resolution screen.
UNPLOT : Removes a point from the high resolution screen.
APND : Loads a BASIC program into memory at a certain address.
PROG : Goes to a BASIC program at a specified address.
OLD : OLDS a NEWed program.
MSAVE : Saves a specified area of memory.
MLOAD : Loads a program into a specified area of memory.
MVERIFY : Verifies a program from a specified area of memory.
INVERT : Inverts an area of memory.
OFF : Turns off NEW BASIC and returns to normal BASIC.

Before we start altering anything, though, we must copy the BASIC ROM to the RAM directly behind it. This is far too slow in BASIC, so use the following machine code program:

```
CØØØ  AØ  ØØ        LDY  #$ØØ
CØØ2  A9  ØØ        LDA  #$ØØ
```

109

```
C004 85 FB          STA  $FB
C006 A9 A0          LDA  #$A0
C008 85 FC          STA  $FC
C00A B1 FB          LDA  ($FB),Y
C00C 91 FB          STA  ($FB),Y
C00E C8             INY
C00F D0 F9          BNE  $C00A
C011 E6 FC          INC  $FC
C013 A5 FC          LDA  $FC
C015 C9 C0          CMP  #$C0
C017 90 F1          BCC  $C00A
C019 60             RTS
```

To make the necessary changes for the computer to operate in the RAM BASIC, all that is required is to switch out ROM BASIC and switch RAM BASIC in. This is done if you POKE 1,54.

A BASIC keyword is stored as ASCII characters, with the last character having bit seven set to tell the computer that the end of the keyword has been reached, eg. the command 'END' is stored in memory like this:

69	e	
78	n	
196	D	(ASCII of d + 128)

Therefore, to make our keyword work we must change the values in these locations; we must also keep the keyword the same length and set bit seven of the last letter. To change the command 'END' to 'CLG' the following values must replace the above:

67	c	
76	l	
199	G	(ASCII of g + 128)

The keywords are stored in the BASIC ROM from locations $A09E to $A19D, and the vectors for the routines that they jump to are located from $A00C to $A09D. They list as follows:

KEY-WORD	LOCATION OF KEYWORD	VECTOR STORED AT	ROUTINE
enD	41118–41120	40972–40973	43056
foR	41121–41123	40974–40975	42817
nexT	41124–41127	40976–40977	44317
datA	41128–41131	40978–40979	43255
input#	41132–41137	40980–40981	43940
inpuT	41138–41142	40982–40983	43966
diM	41143–41145	40984–40985	45184
reaD	41146–41149	40986–40987	44037
leT	41150–41152	40988–40989	43428
gotO	41153–41156	40990–40991	43167
ruN	41157–41159	40992–40993	43120
iF	41160–41161	40994–40995	43303
restorE	41162–41168	40996–40997	43036
gosuB	41169–41173	40998–40999	43138
returN	41174–41179	41000–41001	43217
reM	41180–41182	41002–41003	43322
stoP	41183–41186	41004–41005	43054
oN	41187–41188	41006–41007	43338
waiT	41189–41190	41008–41009	47148
loaD	41193–41196	41010–41011	57703
savE	41197–41200	41012–41013	57685
verify	41201–41206	41014–41015	57700
deF	41207–41209	41016–41017	46002
pokE	41210–41213	41018–41019	47139
print#	41214–41219	41020–41021	43647
prinT	41120–41124	41122–41123	43679
conT	41125–41128	41024–41025	43094
lisT	41129–41132	41026–41027	42651
clR	41233–41235	41028–41029	42589
cmD	41236–41238	41030–41031	43653
syS	41239–41241	41032–41033	57641
opeN	41242–41245	41034–41035	57789
closE	41246–41250	41036–41037	57798
geT	41251–41253	41038–41039	43898
neW	41254–41256	41040–41041	42561
tab(	41257–41260	41042–41043	48185
tO	41261–41262	41044–41045	48332
fN	41263–41264	41046–41047	48216
spc(	41265–41266	41048–41049	784
theN	41269–41272	41050–41051	45949
noT	41273–41275	41052–41053	45982
steP	41276–41279	41054–41055	49009

To change the address that the command goes to when executed, all you need to do is to change the address in lo-/hi-byte order in the locations stated above. For example, we will change the 'END' command (now 'CLG') to go to 49152. The lo-byte of 49152 is zero and the hi-byte is 192 (0+256*192 = 49152).

The vector for the 'END' command is at locations 40972 and 40973 ($A00C and $A00D). Therefore, to make the 'END' command go to 49152 when called, you must POKE (or LDA/STA) 40972 with zero and 40973 with 192. Now when you type 'END' (or 'CLG' if you have changed the command), the computer will jump to 49152. (Remember to turn on the NEW BASIC with POKE 1,54.)

To demonstrate this, we will now add our first command to BASIC. . .GRAPH. I will demonstrate this by going through every step. (This procedure should not be necessary for each command.)

Firstly write the code. We will use the same code for SYS GRAPH as in the *high resolution graphics* section. The only change needed to any of the commands in the previous section is that we miss out the first comma (check if there is one). The code is therefore as follows:

```
A C000 LDA #$16

A C002 STA $DD00

A C005 LDA #$08

A C007 STA $D018

A C00A LDA $D011

A C00D ORA #$20

A C00F STA $D011

A C012 RTS
```

Now we need to replace a command with the command 'GRAPH'. The command that we replace the ROM command with must be the same length or greater than our new command. For this example, we will use the command 'CLOSE'. The data for this keyword is stored from locations 41246–41250. Therefore, we replace the characters with the following data:

g   71
r   82
a   65
p   80
H   200

Now we need to change the address that the command goes to when called; these addresses, according to the above chart, are 41036 and 41037. So we put the lo-byte (zero) into 40136 and the hi-byte (192) into 40137.

Now, if you type 'GRAPH' the high resolution screen will be turned on. To get back to the text screen, type SYS 49152+19 if you have the 'norm' machine code in memory (otherwise, press Run/Stop and Restore).

Let us now add a command that needs parameters—for example, 'CLG'. I will replace the command 'DEF' with 'CLG'. 'DEF' is located from locations 41207–41209, so we POKE the following values into 41207–41209:

67   c
76   l
199   G (71+128)

Now we need to change the values in the vector that the command is called from. These values are located from 41016–41017. The CLG routine is located at 49187, so we POKE 41016 with 35 (the lo-byte) and 41017 with 192 (the hi-byte), ie. 49187÷256 = 192.1337. So the hi-byte is 192. Now multiply the remainder by 256, i.e. .1337*256 = 35.

The SYS CLG routine starts with a 'JSR $AEFD' command. This is just to separate the number after the SYS from the parameters coming after. As the commands we are using have no numbers in their keywords, we do not need this comma check. The CLG routine is as follows:

```
C023 20 8A AD        JSR  $AD8A
C026 20 F7 B7        JSR  $B7F7
C029 A5 15           LDA  $15
C02B F0 03           BEQ  $C030
C02D 4C 48 B2        JMP  $B248
C030 A5 14           LDA  $14
C032 8D 7F C0        STA  $C07F
C035 20 FD AE        JSR  $AEFD
C038 20 8A AD        JSR  $AD8A
C03B 20 F7 B7        JSR  $B7F7
C03E A5 15           LDA  $15
C040 F0 03           BEQ  $C045
C042 4C 48 B2        JMP  $B248
C045 A5 14           LDA  $14
C047 0A              ASL
C048 0A              ASL
C049 0A              ASL
C04A 0A              ASL
C04B 0D 7F C0        ORA  $C07F
C04E 8D 7F C0        STA  $C07F
C051 A9 00           LDA  #$00
C053 85 FB           STA  $FB
C055 A9 60           LDA  #$60
C057 85 FC           STA  $FC
C059 A0 00           LDY  #$00
C05B A9 00           LDA  #$00
C05D 91 FB           STA  ($FB),Y
C05F C8              INY
C060 D0 FB           BNE  $C05D
C062 E6 FC           INC  $FC
C064 A6 FC           LDX  $FC
C066 E0 80           CPX  #$80
C068 D0 F3           BNE  $C05D
C06A AD 7F C0        LDA  $C07F
C06D A2 00           LDX  #$00
```

114

```
CØ6F 9D ØØ 4Ø        STA $4ØØØ,X
CØ72 9D ØØ 41        STA $41ØØ,X
CØ75 9D ØØ 42        STA $42ØØ,X
CØ78 9D ØØ 43        STA $43ØØ,X
CØ7B E8              INX
CØ7C DØ F1           BNE $CØ6F
CØ7E 6Ø              RTS
```

To clear the screen using 'CLG', type CLG background colour, line colour (where the colours are the usual Commodore numbers, i.e. Ø=black, 7=yellow, etc.)

Now we will add the rest of the commands as one, and use a short BASIC program to enter the commands and their vectors into RAM. The BASIC will also contain the ROM to RAM routine shown earlier in this section. The way to type this in is to type in all the machine code into the computer and save it using *SUPERMON*. Then type in and save the BASIC program. Now, RUN the BASIC program. The program will load the machine code from tape or disk depending upon which you specify by altering the line number in line Ø.

```
CØØØ A9 16           LDA #$16
CØØ2 8D ØØ DD        STA $DDØØ
CØØ5 A9 Ø8           LDA #$Ø8
CØØ7 8D 18 DØ        STA $DØ18
CØØA AD 11 DØ        LDA $DØ11
CØØD Ø9 2Ø           ORA #$2Ø
CØØF 8D 11 DØ        STA $DØ11
CØ12 6Ø              RTS
CØ13 A9 15           LDA #$15
CØ15 8D 18 DØ        STA $DØ18
CØ18 A9 1B           LDA #$1B
CØ1A 8D 11 DØ        STA $DØ11
CØ1D A9 17           LDA #$17
CØ1F 8D ØØ DD        STA $DDØØ
CØ22 6Ø              RTS
CØ23 2Ø 8A AD        JSR $AD8A
CØ26 2Ø F7 B7        JSR $B7F7
CØ29 A5 15           LDA $15
CØ2B FØ Ø3           BEQ $CØ3Ø
```

115

```
CØ2D 4C 48 B2     JMP $B248
CØ3Ø A5 14        LDA $14
CØ32 8D 7F CØ     STA $CØ7F
CØ35 2Ø FD AE     JSR $AEFD
CØ38 2Ø 8A AD     JSR $AD8A
CØ3B 2Ø F7 B7     JSR $B7F7
CØ3E A5 15        LDA $15
CØ4Ø FØ Ø3        BEQ $CØ45
CØ42 4C 48 B2     JMP $B248
CØ45 A5 14        LDA $14
CØ47 ØA           ASL
CØ48 ØA           ASL
CØ49 ØA           ASL
CØ4A ØA           ASL
CØ4B ØD 7F CØ     ORA $CØ7F
CØ4E 8D 7F CØ     STA $CØ7F
CØ51 A9 ØØ        LDA #$ØØ
CØ53 85 FB        STA $FB
CØ55 A9 6Ø        LDA #$6Ø
CØ57 85 FC        STA $FC
CØ59 AØ ØØ        LDY #$ØØ
CØ5B A9 ØØ        LDA #$ØØ
CØ5D 91 FB        STA ($FB),Y
CØ5F C8           INY
CØ6Ø DØ FB        BNE $CØ5D
CØ62 E6 FC        INC $FC
CØ64 A6 FC        LDX $FC
CØ66 EØ 8Ø        CPX #$8Ø
CØ68 DØ F3        BNE $CØ5D
CØ6A AD 7F CØ     LDA $CØ7F
CØ6D A2 ØØ        LDX #$ØØ
CØ6F 9D ØØ 4Ø     STA $4ØØØ,X
CØ72 9D ØØ 41     STA $41ØØ,X
CØ75 9D ØØ 42     STA $42ØØ,X
CØ78 9D ØØ 43     STA $43ØØ,X
CØ7B E8           INX
CØ7C DØ F1        BNE $CØ6F
CØ7E 6Ø           RTS
CØ7F ØØ           BRK
CØ8Ø 2Ø 8A AD     JSR $AD8A
```

```
CØ83 2Ø F7 B7      JSR $B7F7
CØ86 A5 14         LDA $14
CØ88 85 FB         STA $FB
CØ8A A5 15         LDA $15
CØ8C 85 FC         STA $FC
CØ8E 2Ø FD AE      JSR $AEFD
CØ91 2Ø 8A AD      JSR $AD8A
CØ94 2Ø F7 B7      JSR $B7F7
CØ97 A5 14         LDA $14
CØ99 8D 3C Ø3      STA $Ø33C
CØ9C A5 15         LDA $15
CØ9E 8D 3D Ø3      STA $Ø33D
CØA1 2Ø FD AE      JSR $AEFD
CØA4 2Ø 8A AD      JSR $AD8A
CØA7 2Ø F7 B7      JSR $B7F7
CØAA A5 15         LDA $15
CØAC FØ Ø3         BEQ $CØB1
CØAE 4C 48 B2      JMP $B248
CØB1 A5 14         LDA $14
CØB3 8D 3E Ø3      STA $Ø33E
CØB6 AØ ØØ         LDY #$ØØ
CØB8 AD 3E Ø3      LDA $Ø33E
CØBB 91 FB         STA ($FB),Y
CØBD 2Ø D4 CØ      JSR $CØD4
CØCØ A5 FB         LDA $FB
CØC2 CD 3C Ø3      CMP $Ø33C
CØC5 FØ Ø3         BEQ $CØCA
CØC7 4C B6 CØ      JMP $CØB6
CØCA A5 FC         LDA $FC
CØCC CD 3D Ø3      CMP $Ø33D
CØCF FØ ØB         BEQ $CØDC
CØD1 4C B6 CØ      JMP $CØB6
CØD4 E6 FB         INC $FB
CØD6 FØ Ø1         BEQ $CØD9
CØD8 6Ø            RTS
CØD9 E6 FC         INC $FC
CØDB 6Ø            RTS
CØDC 6Ø            RTS
CØDD 2Ø 1D C1      JSR $C11D
CØEØ A5 14         LDA $14
```

```
C0E2 8D 21 D0    STA $D021
C0E5 20 FD AE    JSR $AEFD
C0E8 20 1D C1    JSR $C11D
C0EB A5 14       LDA $14
C0ED 8D 20 D0    STA $D020
C0F0 20 FD AE    JSR $AEFD
C0F3 20 1D C1    JSR $C11D
C0F6 A5 14       LDA $14
C0F8 8D 86 02    STA $0286
C0FB 20 FD AE    JSR $AEFD
C0FE 20 1D C1    JSR $C11D
C101 A5 14       LDA $14
C103 8D 22 D0    STA $D022
C106 20 FD AE    JSR $AEFD
C109 20 1D C1    JSR $C11D
C10C A5 14       LDA $14
C10E 8D 23 D0    STA $D023
C111 20 FD AE    JSR $AEFD
C114 20 1D C1    JSR $C11D
C117 A5 14       LDA $14
C119 8D 24 D0    STA $D024
C11C 60          RTS
C11D 20 8A AD    JSR $AD8A
C120 20 F7 B7    JSR $B7F7
C123 A5 15       LDA $15
C125 D0 01       BNE $C128
C127 60          RTS
C128 4C 48 B2    JMP $B248
C12B A9 FF       LDA #$FF
C12D D0 02       BNE $C131
C12F A9 00       LDA #$00
C131 8D DC C1    STA $C1DC
C134 20 EB B7    JSR $B7EB
C137 E0 C8       CPX #$C8
C139 B0 5E       BCS $C199
C13B A5 14       LDA $14
C13D C9 40       CMP #$40
C13F A5 15       LDA $15
C141 E9 01       SBC #$01
C143 B0 54       BCS $C199
```

```
C145 8A              TXA
C146 4A              LSR
C147 4A              LSR
C148 4A              LSR
C149 ØA              ASL
C14A A8              TAY
C14B B9 9A C1        LDA $C19A,Y
C14E 85 FD           STA $FD
C150 B9 9B C1        LDA $C19B,Y
C153 85 FE           STA $FE
C155 8A              TXA
C156 29 Ø7           AND #$Ø7
C158 18              CLC
C159 65 FD           ADC $FD
C15B 85 FD           STA $FD
C15D A5 FE           LDA $FE
C15F 69 ØØ           ADC #$ØØ
C161 85 FE           STA $FE
C163 A5 14           LDA $14
C165 29 Ø7           AND #$Ø7
C167 A8              TAY
C168 A5 14           LDA $14
C16A 29 F8           AND #$F8
C16C 18              CLC
C16D 65 FD           ADC $FD
C16F 85 FD           STA $FD
C171 A5 FE           LDA $FE
C173 65 15           ADC $15
C175 85 FE           STA $FE
C177 A5 FD           LDA $FD
C179 18              CLC
C17A 69 ØØ           ADC #$ØØ
C17C 85 FD           STA $FD
C17E A5 FE           LDA $FE
C180 69 6Ø           ADC #$6Ø
C182 85 FE           STA $FE
C184 A2 ØØ           LDX #$ØØ
C186 A1 FD           LDA ($FD,X)
C188 2C DC C1        BIT $C1DC
C18B 1Ø Ø6           BPL $C193
```

```
C18D 39 D4 C1        AND $C1D4,Y
C190 4C 96 C1        JMP $C196
C193 19 CC C1        ORA $C1CC,Y
C196 81 FD           STA ($FD,X)
C198 60              RTS
C199 60              RTS
 .


 .
.:C19A 00 00 40 01 80 02 C0 03
.:C1A2 00 05 40 06 80 07 C0 08
.:C1AA 00 0A 40 0B 80 0C C0 0D
.:C1B2 00 0F 40 10 80 11 C0 12
.:C1BA 00 14 40 15 80 16 C0 17
.:C1C2 00 19 40 1A 80 1B C0 1C
.:C1CA 00 1E 80 40 20 10 08 04
.:C1D2 02 01 7F BF DF EF F7 FB
.:C1DA FD FE 00 4C 48 B2 20 BC


C1DD 4C 48 B2        JMP $B248
C1E0 20 BC C2        JSR $C2BC
C1E3 A5 14           LDA $14
C1E5 C9 28           CMP #$28
C1E7 B0 F4           BCS $C1DD
C1E9 8D EA C2        STA $C2EA
C1EC 20 FD AE        JSR $AEFD
C1EF 20 BC C2        JSR $C2BC
C1F2 A5 14           LDA $14
C1F4 C9 19           CMP #$19
C1F6 B0 E5           BCS $C1DD
C1F8 8D EB C2        STA $C2EB
C1FB AD EA C2        LDA $C2EA
C1FE 8D E7 C2        STA $C2E7
C201 A9 08           LDA #$08
C203 8D E8 C2        STA $C2E8
C206 20 CA C2        JSR $C2CA
C209 AD E5 C2        LDA $C2E5
C20C 85 FB           STA $FB
```

```
C20E AD E6 C2        LDA $C2E6
C211 85 FC           STA $FC
C213 AD EB C2        LDA $C2EB
C216 8D E7 C2        STA $C2E7
C219 A9 28           LDA #$28
C21B 8D E8 C2        STA $C2E8
C21E 20 CA C2        JSR $C2CA
C221 AD E5 C2        LDA $C2E5
C224 8D EF C2        STA $C2EF
C227 AD E6 C2        LDA $C2E6
C22A 8D F0 C2        STA $C2F0
C22D A2 07           LDX #$07
C22F AD E5 C2        LDA $C2E5
C232 6D EF C2        ADC $C2EF
C235 8D E5 C2        STA $C2E5
C238 AD E6 C2        LDA $C2E6
C23B 69 00           ADC #$00
C23D 8D E6 C2        STA $C2E6
C240 CA              DEX
C241 D0 EC           BNE $C22F
C243 A2 07           LDX #$07
C245 AD E6 C2        LDA $C2E6
C248 18              CLC
C249 6D F0 C2        ADC $C2F0
C24C 8D E6 C2        STA $C2E6
C24F CA              DEX
C250 D0 F3           BNE $C245
C252 AD E6 C2        LDA $C2E6
C255 18              CLC
C256 69 60           ADC #$60
C258 8D E6 C2        STA $C2E6
C25B A5 FB           LDA $FB
C25D 18              CLC
C25E 6D E5 C2        ADC $C2E5
C261 85 FB           STA $FB
C263 A5 FC           LDA $FC
C265 6D E6 C2        ADC $C2E6
C268 85 FC           STA $FC
C26A 20 FD AE        JSR $AEFD
C26D 20 BC C2        JSR $C2BC
```

```
C270 A5 14          LDA $14
C272 8D ED C2       STA $C2ED
C275 AD ED C2       LDA $C2ED
C278 8D E7 C2       STA $C2E7
C27B A9 08          LDA #$08
C27D 8D E8 C2       STA $C2E8
C280 20 CA C2       JSR $C2CA
C283 AD E5 C2       LDA $C2E5
C286 85 FD          STA $FD
C288 AD E6 C2       LDA $C2E6
C28B 18             CLC
C28C 69 D0          ADC #$D0
C28E 85 FE          STA $FE
C290 A9 00          LDA #$00
C292 8D E9 C2       STA $C2E9
C295 78             SEI
C296 A9 33          LDA #$33
C298 85 01          STA $01
C29A A0 00          LDY #$00
C29C B1 FD          LDA ($FD),Y
C29E 91 FB          STA ($FB),Y
C2A0 E6 FB          INC $FB
C2A2 D0 02          BNE $C2A6
C2A4 E6 FC          INC $FC
C2A6 E6 FD          INC $FD
C2A8 D0 02          BNE $C2AC
C2AA E6 FE          INC $FE
C2AC EE E9 C2       INC $C2E9
C2AF AD E9 C2       LDA $C2E9
C2B2 C9 08          CMP #$08
C2B4 D0 E6          BNE $C29C
C2B6 A9 37          LDA #$37
C2B8 85 01          STA $01
C2BA 58             CLI
C2BB 60             RTS
C2BC 20 8A AD       JSR $AD8A
C2BF 20 F7 B7       JSR $B7F7
C2C2 A5 15          LDA $15
C2C4 F0 03          BEQ $C2C9
C2C6 4C 48 B2       JMP $B248
```

```
C2C9 60              RTS
C2CA A9 00           LDA #$00
C2CC 8D E5 C2        STA $C2E5
C2CF A2 08           LDX #$08
C2D1 4E E7 C2        LSR $C2E7
C2D4 90 04           BCC $C2DA
C2D6 18              CLC
C2D7 6D E8 C2        ADC $C2E8
C2DA 6A              ROR
C2DB 6E E5 C2        ROR $C2E5
C2DE CA              DEX
C2DF D0 F0           BNE $C2D1
C2E1 8D E6 C2        STA $C2E6
C2E4 60              RTS
C2E5 00              BRK
C2E6 00              BRK
C2E7 00              BRK
C2E8 00              BRK
C2E9 00              BRK
C2EA 00              BRK
C2EB 00              BRK
C2EC 00              BRK
C2ED 00              BRK
C2EE 00              BRK
C2EF 00              BRK
C2F0 00              BRK
C2F1 20 8A AD        JSR $AD8A
C2F4 20 F7 B7        JSR $B7F7
C2F7 A5 14           LDA $14
C2F9 85 FB           STA $FB
C2FB A5 15           LDA $15
C2FD 85 FC           STA $FC
C2FF 20 FD AE        JSR $AEFD
C302 20 8A AD        JSR $AD8A
C305 20 F7 B7        JSR $B7F7
C308 A5 14           LDA $14
C30A 8D 3C 03        STA $033C
C30D A5 15           LDA $15
C30F 8D 3D 03        STA $033D
C312 A0 00           LDY #$00
```

123

```
C314 A9 FF        LDA #$FF
C316 51 FB        EOR ($FB),Y
C318 91 FB        STA ($FB),Y
C31A 20 31 C3     JSR $C331
C31D A5 FB        LDA $FB
C31F CD 3C 03     CMP $033C
C322 F0 03        BEQ $C327
C324 4C 12 C3     JMP $C312
C327 A5 FC        LDA $FC
C329 CD 3D 03     CMP $033D
C32C F0 0B        BEQ $C339
C32E 4C 12 C3     JMP $C312
C331 E6 FB        INC $FB
C333 F0 01        BEQ $C336
C335 60           RTS
C336 E6 FC        INC $FC
C338 60           RTS
C339 60           RTS
C33A A9 37        LDA #$37
C33C 85 01        STA $01
C33E 60           RTS
C33F A9 FF        LDA #$FF
C341 A0 01        LDY #$01
C343 91 2B        STA ($2B),Y
C345 20 33 A5     JSR $A533
C348 A5 22        LDA $22
C34A 18           CLC
C34B 69 02        ADC #$02
C34D 85 2D        STA $2D
C34F A5 23        LDA $23
C351 69 00        ADC #$00
C353 85 2E        STA $2E
C355 4C 5E A6     JMP $A65E
C358 20 D4 E1     JSR $E1D4
C35B 20 FD AE     JSR $AEFD
C35E 20 8A AD     JSR $AD8A
C361 20 F7 B7     JSR $B7F7
C364 A5 14        LDA $14
C366 48           PHA
C367 A5 15        LDA $15
```

```
C369 48              PHA
C36A 20 FD AE        JSR $AEFD
C36D 20 8A AD        JSR $AD8A
C370 20 F7 B7        JSR $B7F7
C373 A6 14           LDX $14
C375 A4 15           LDY $15
C377 68              PLA
C378 85 FC           STA $FC
C37A 68              PLA
C37B 85 FB           STA $FB
C37D A9 FB           LDA #$FB
C37F 4C 5F E1        JMP $E15F
C382 A9 01           LDA #$01
C384 85 0A           STA $0A
C386 4C 8D C3        JMP $C38D
C389 A9 00           LDA #$00
C38B 85 0A           STA $0A
C38D 20 D4 E1        JSR $E1D4
C390 20 FD AE        JSR $AEFD
C393 20 8A AD        JSR $AD8A
C396 20 F7 B7        JSR $B7F7
C399 A5 0A           LDA $0A
C39B A6 14           LDX $14
C39D A4 15           LDY $15
C39F 4C 75 E1        JMP $E175
C3A2 20 FD AE        JSR $AEFD
C3A5 20 D4 E1        JSR $E1D4
C3A8 A9 00           LDA #$00
C3AA A6 2D           LDX $2D
C3AC A4 2E           LDY $2E
C3AE 4C 75 E1        JMP $E175
C3B1 EA              NOP
C3B2 A5 2E           LDA $2E
C3B4 A6 2D           LDX $2D
C3B6 20 CD BD        JSR $BDCD
C3B9 4C 33 A5        JMP $A533
C3BC A5 2E           LDA $2E
C3BE A6 2D           LDX $2D
C3C0 20 CD BD        JSR $BDCD
C3C3 4C 33 A5        JMP $A533
```

```
0  ifx=0thenx=1:load"basicode",8,1
10 a=0
20 readb:ifb=-1then130
30 poke32768+a,b
40 a=a+1:goto20
70 data 160,0,169,0,133,251
80 data 169,160,133,252
90 data 177,251,145,251,200
100 data 208,249,230,252
110 data 165,252,201,192
120 data 144,241,96,-1
130 sys32768
140 reada,b:ifa=-1then200
150 hi=int(b/256):lo=((b/256)-hi)*256
160 pokea,lo:pokea+1,hi
170 goto140
200 reada,a$
205 ifa=-1then300
210 forb=1tolen(a$)
220 c=asc(mid$(a$,b,1))
230 pokea+b-1,c
240 next
250 goto200
300 print"new basic enabled"
310 poke1,54:end
1000 rem graph = input
1010 data 40982,49151
1020 rem nrm = dim
1030 data 40984,49170
1040 rem clg = let
1050 data 40988,49186
1060 rem fill = save
1070 data 41012,49279
1080 rem colour = print#
1090 data 41020,49372
1100 rem plot = wait
1110 data 41008,49454
1120 rem unplot = input#
1130 data 40980,49450
1140 rem char = cont
```

```
1150 data 41024,49631
1160 rem invert = verify
1170 data 41014,49904
1180 rem off = run
1190 data 40992,49977
1200 rem old = def
1210 data 41016,49982
1220 rem msave = print
1230 data 41022,50007
1240 rem mload = close
1250 data 41036,50056
1260 rem mverify= restore
1270 data 40996,50049
1280 rem apnd = tab(
1290 data 41042,50081
1300 rem prog = stop
1310 data 41004,50107
1320 data -1,-1
1330 :
1500 data 41138,"grapH"
1510 data 41143,"nrM"
1520 data 41150,"clG"
1530 data 41197,"filL"
1540 data 41214,"colouR"
1550 data 41189,"ploT"
1560 data 41132,"unploT"
1570 data 41225,"chaR"
1580 data 41201,"inverT"
1590 data 41157,"ofF"
1600 data 41207,"olD"
1610 data 41220,"msavE"
1620 data 41246,"mloaD"
1630 data 41162,"mverifY"
1640 data 41257,"apnD"
1650 data 41183,"proG"
1660 data-1,-1
```

Once you have RUN the BASIC program the new keywords will be in place and ready for use. Here is a list of all the commands, what they are used for and what their syntax is.

GRAPH   : Turns on the high resolution screen (syntax . . . GRAPH).

NRM   : Turns off the high resolution screen (syntax . . . NRM).

CLG   : Clears and colours the high resolution screen (syntax . . . CLG background colour, foreground colour).

FILL   : Fills memory with a byte (syntax . . . FILL start, finish, byte).

COLOUR   : Sets the screen, border, text and multi1, 2 and 3 colours (syntax . . . COLOUR screen, border, text, multi1, multi2, multi3).

PLOT   : Plots a point on the high resolution screen (syntax . . . PLOT X,Y—where 'X' is from zero to 319 and 'Y' is from zero to 199).

UNPLOT   : Removes a point from the high resolution screen (syntax . . . UNPLOT X,Y—the same restrictions apply as with PLOT).

CHAR   : Puts an eight by eight character on the high resolution screen in the text format (syntax . . . CHAR X,Y, character—where 'X' is from zero to 39, 'Y' is from zero to 24 and 'character' is the POKE code of the character from zero to 255).

INVERT   : Inverts an area of memory (EORs it with #$FF). On the high resolution screen this turns every 'on' pixel off and every 'off' pixel on (syntax . . . INVERT start, finish).

OFF   : Turns off NEW BASIC and returns to normal BASIC (syntax . . . OFF).

OLD   : Restores a BASIC program inadvertently NEWed. This will only work if no variables have been defined before the NEW, and no program lines have been entered (syntax . . . OLD).

MSAVE   : Saves an area of memory onto tape or disk. This can be loaded with the 'MLOAD' command or LOAD"name", device,1 (syntax . . . MSAVE"name", device, 1, start, address+1).

MLOAD   : Loads a program from disk or tape into memory starting at the location specified (syntax . . . MLOAD"name", device, 1, start).

MVERIFY   : Verifies a program on tape or disk with the one in memory starting with the location specified (syntax . . . MVERIFY"name", device, 1, start).

APPEND   : This routine allows you to load a number of BASIC programs into memory at once and using the 'PROG' command, access each one individually. The program raises the bottom of memory each time the next program is called. To find out the address use the 'PROG' command to find the start address of the program and POKE 43 with the lo-byte and 44 with the hi-byte (syntax . . . APPEND"name", device,0).

PROG   : This command tells you the starting address of the BASIC program just loaded into memory. It must also be used before RUNning a BASIC program in memory as it tells you the address of the BASIC program and re-chains the BASIC lines so that the computer can understand what the lines mean.

If you press the Run/Stop key and the RESTORE key together at any time and you want to use the new commands again, you must type POKE 1,54.

Here are a couple of programs that demonstrate the use of the new commands. The first one is a demo, and the second allows you to draw a picture on the screen. instructions are included within the programs.

Type them in exactly as listed with the new BASIC in operation. Some of the commands (especially 'MSAVE') look as if their syntax could be wrong in the listing. Don't panic—this is because the program was listed with the *new*

BASIC in operation and 'MSAVE' is 'PRINT' in normal BASIC.

```
10 POKE1,55:MSAVE"{CLR}"
20 MSAVE:MSAVE:MSAVE"DEMO OF NEW BASIC C
OMMANDS"
30 POKE1,54
40 FORA=ØTO15:FORB=ØTO15
50 COLOURA,B,Ø,1,1,1
60 NEXTB,A
65 COLOUR 1,3,2,1,1,1
70 OFF:MSAVE"{CLR}":POKE1,54
80 FILL 1024,2023,81
90 FORA=ØTO255STEP4
100 FILL 55296,56295,A
110 NEXT
120 OFF:MSAVE"{CLR}":MSAVE:MSAVE
125 MSAVE"{CUR RT} HIRES GRAPHICS !!!"
130 MSAVE"THE SCREEN CAN BE ANY OF 255 C
OLOUR     COMBINATIONS"
140 :MSAVE:MSAVE:MSAVE"WATCH":FORR=ØTO20
ØØ:NEXT
150 POKE1,54
160 GRAPH:FORA=ØTO15:FORB=ØTO15
170 CLGB,A:NEXTB,A
180 COLOUR Ø,2,7,1,1,1
190 CLG Ø,7
200 OFF:MSAVE"{CLR}CIRCLES,SINES AND LINES!"
:{GY 1}1,54
210 FORA=ØTO39:CHAR A,1,PEEK(1024+A):NEX
T:OFF:MSAVE"{CLR}NOW YOU SEE IT!"
230 POKE1,54:FORA=ØTO15:CHAR8+A,10,PEEK(
1024+A):NEXT
240 FORA=ØTO319:PLOT A,84:NEXT
250 FORR=ØTO1000:NEXT
260 FORA=ØTO319:UNPLOT A,84:NEXT
270 OFF:MSAVE"{CLR}NOW YOU DON'T!!!"
280 POKE1,54:FORA=ØTO15:CHAR8+A,10,PEEK(
1024+A):NEXT
290 FORR=ØTO1000:NEXT
```

```
300 COLOUR1,3,2,1,1,1
310 CLG1,2
320 C=110:D=100
330 FORA=0TO6.5STEP0.01
340 X=C*SIN(A)+160:Y=D*COS(A)+100
350 PLOTX,Y
360 NEXT
370 FORR=0TO1000:NEXT
380 INVERT24576,32768
390 FORR=0TO1000:NEXT
400 INVERT24576,32768
410 FORR=0TO2000:NEXT
420 NRM:OFF:MSAVE"{CLR}"
423 MSAVE:MSAVE:MSAVE"{CUR RT}{CUR RT}";
425 MSAVE"I HAVE JUST NEWED THE PROGRAM.
  TO        CONTINUE"
430 MSAVE"THE PROGRAM TYPE OLD AND GOTO
450
440 POKE1,54:NEW
450 OFF:MSAVE"{CLR}THANK YOU!":POKE1,54
460 FORR=0TO1000:NEXT:GRAPH
470 C=110:D=100
480 FORA=0TO6.5STEP0.01
490 X=C*SIN(A)+160:Y=D*COS(A)+100
500 UNPLOTX,Y
510 NEXT:NRM
520 OFF:MSAVE"{CLR}{CUR DN}{CUR DN}{CUR RT}";
525 MSAVE"DO YOU WANT TO SEE THE DEMO AG
AIN?"
530 GRAPHA$:IFA$="N"ORA$="Y"THEN550
540 GOTO530
550 OFF


0 IFDX=1THEN2420
1 IFDX=2THEN2430
2 UNVAR=1:MV=1:X=160:Y=100
3 POKE1,54
4 COLOUR 1,3,2,1,1,1
5 OFF
6 POKE650,128
```

```
10 MSAVE"{CLR}"
20 MSAVE" THIS PROGRAM ALLOWS YOU TO DRA
W         PICTURES ON THE SCREEN"
30 MSAVE"USING THE FOLLOWING KEYS"
40 MSAVE
50 MSAVE"  Z = LEFT       X = RIGHT"
60 MSAVE"  ; = UP         / = DOWN"
70 MSAVE:MSAVE"PRESS F1 TO PLOT AND F7 T
O UNPLOT"
80 MSAVE"IN PLOT MODE A 1 WILL BE DISPLA
YED IN TEH TOP LEFT OF THE SCREEN"
90 MSAVE"IN UNPLOT MODE A ZERO WILL BE D
ISPLAYED"
100 MSAVE"PRESS ← (BACK ARROW FOR THE HE
LP LIST"
110 MSAVE"PRESS A KEY TO BEGIN"
120 POKE198,0:PLOT198,1
130 MSAVE"{CLR}"
140 GRAPH"SCREEN COLOUR";S
150 GRAPH"BORDER COLOUR";B
160 GRAPH"LINE COLOUR";L
165 POKE1,54
170 COLOUR S,B,L,1,1,1
180 CLGS,L
190 GRAPH
195 POKE 16384,16*S+L
200 CHAR0,0,49
210 REM MAIN LOOP
220 GETA$:IFA$="←"THEN1000
230 IFA$="Z"THENX=X-MV
240 IFA$="X"THENX=X+MV
250 IFA$=";"THENY=Y-MV
260 IFA$="/"THENY=Y+MV
270 IFA$="§"THENUNVAR=1:CHAR0,0,49
280 IFA$="THENUNVAR=0:CHAR0,0,48
290 IFUNVAR=1THENPLOTX,Y
300 IFUNVAR=0THENUNPLOTX,Y
310 GOTO220
1000 NRM:OFF
1010 MSAVE"{CLR}"
```

```
1020 MSAVE"OPTIONS"
1030 MSAVE"1: CLEAR SCREEN"
1040 MSAVE"2: CHANGE COLOURS"
1060 MSAVE"3: SAVE SCREEN"
1070 MSAVE"4: LOAD SCREEN"
1080 MSAVE"5: INVERT SCREEN"
1090 MSAVE"6: QUIT"
1095 GETA$:IFA$=""THEN1095
1100 IFVAL(A$)<0ORVAL(A$)>7THEN1010
1110 ONVAL(A$)GOTO2000,2100,2300,2400,25
00,2600
1120 GOTO1010
2000 POKE1,54:CLGS,L
2010 GRAPH:GOTO220
2100 GRAPH"SCREEN COLOUR";S
2110 GRAPH"BORDER COLOUR";B
2120 GRAPH"PLOTTING COLOUR";L
2130 POKE1,54:COLOUR S,B,L,1,1,1:FILL 16
384,17384,L*16+S
2140 GRAPH:GOTO220
2300 GRAPH"DEVICE";DN
2310 POKE1,54
2320 MSAVE"SCREEN1",DN,1,16384,17383
2330 MSAVE"SCREEN2",DN,1,24576,32768
2340 GRAPH:GOTO220
2400 GRAPH"DEVICE";DN
2410 POKE1,54:DX=1:MLOAD"SCREEN1",DN,1,1
6384
2420 DX=2:MLOAD"SCREEN2",DN,1,24576
2430 GRAPH:GOTO220
2500 POKE1,54:INVERT24576,32768
2510 GRAPH:GOTO220
2600 GRAPH"ARE YOU SURE";S$
2610 IFLEFT$(S$,1)="Y"THENEND
2620 GOTO1000
```

SECTION 3

ROM ROUTINES AND THE KERNAL

This section covers the ROMs inside the '64. It explains what and where the routines are and if they can be used in a user's program, how to use them and what function they perform, and what values they return.

We will start with the BASIC ROM, which is located from $A000 (40960) to $BFFF (49151).

THE BASIC ROM

The format for each explanation is as follows:

Label, Location in Hex . . . Description and usage.

BCOLD $A000–$A001 : BASIC cold start vector. These two bytes contain the value for a cold start—they jump to $E394 (58260). To do a cold start from BASIC, type SYS 53260 and from machine code JMP $E394.

BWARM $A002–$A003 : BASIC warm start vector. These two bytes contain the value for a warm start—they jump to $e37B (58235). To do a warm start from BASIC, type SYS 58235 and from machine code JMP $E37B.

STMDSP $A004–$A00B : Data for computer. Unfortunately, this is of little use to the programmer.

FUNDSP $A00C–$A051 : BASIC command vector table. This area holds the jump vectors for BASIC commands in lo-byte/hi-byte order. For usage see Section on adding commands to BASIC.

OPTAB $A052–$A079 : BASIC function vector table. This area holds the jump vectors for the BASIC functions in lo-/hi-byte order. For the addresses, see the memory map.

RESLST $A080–$A09D : BASIC operator vector and priority table. This area holds the jump addresses and the priority values for the BASIC operators.

MSCLST $A09E–$A13F	: BASIC command table. This area holds the data for the keywords. For use, see the section on adding commands to BASIC.
OPLIST $A140–$A14C	: BASIC operator table. This area holds the data for the operators.
FUNLST $A14D–$A19E	: BASIC function table. This area holds the data for the BASIC functions.
ERRTAB $A19F–$A327 ·	: Error messages. This area holds the data for the error messages.
ERRPTR $A328–$A363	: Error message pointers. This area holds the pointers for the error messages—it points to where the data for each error message is stored.
OKK $A364–$A389	: Non-error messages. This area holds the data for the non error messages: 'OK', 'ERROR', 'IN', 'READY.' and 'BREAK'.
FNDFOR $A38A–$A3B7	: Finds FOR entry on the stack or skip, and finds the GOSUB entry when called by RETURN.
BLTU $A3B8–$A3B7	: Checks if there is sufficient memory to move a block of memory up and then. . .
BLTUC $A3B8–$A3FA	: Moves the block from the value in LOWTR to HIGHTR–1 up to a new block that ends at HIGHDS-1.
GETSTK $A3FB–$A407	: Checks the stack for space to accommodate a value in A (accumulator) *2 entries. PRINTS an error 'OUT OF MEMORY' message if there is not enough room.

REASON $A408–$A434 : Checks the address in A and Y(A LO,Y HI) is lower than the bottom of string space. If not, then prints the 'OUT OF MEMORY' error message.

OMERR $A435–$A436 : Prints the 'OUT OF MEMORY' error message.

ERROR $A435–$A468 : Prints the error message indicated by the value in X, then. . .

ERRFIN $A469–$A473 : Prints the 'ERROR' or 'BREAK' message if entered from STPEND.

READY $A474–$A47F : BASIC re-start-prints the 'READY' message and then. . .

MAIN $A480–$A4A1 : Inputs a line. Identifies a BASIC line or command.

MAINI $A4A2–$A4A8 : If a BASIC line, then gets the line number and converts keywords in the line to tokens.

INSLIN $A4A9–$A529 : Inserts text from the BASIC buffer into program. Puts the line number into LINNUM on entry. The line must have the keywords changed to tokens and the length of the line in Y. If BBUFF = 0 then the line will be deleted. The routine exists to MAIN.

FINI $A52A–$A532 : After inserting a new line into BASIC text, place into RUNC, LNKPRG and re-enter to MAIN.

LNKPRG $A533–$A55F : Re-chains BASIC lines by re-building BASIC text link pointers.

INLIN $A560–$A578 : Inputs a line into the BASIC buffer and places a zero at the end (a zero indicates the end of a BASIC line).

CRUNCH $A579–$A612 : Changes the keywords to tokens from line in BBUFF to line length. Sets TXTPTR to BBUFF-value in Y. Sets TXTPTR to BBUFF-1 on exit.

FNDLIN $A613–$A617 : Searches BASIC text from the start for a line number in LIN-NUM.

FNDLNC $A617–$A641 : Searches BASIC text from a value in A and Y (a=lo, y=hi) for the line number in LINNUM. If found, sets C and LINPTR points to the start of the line. Else clears C.

SCRATH $A642–$A658 : The NEW command enters here. Checks syntax and then. . .

SCRTCH $A659– : Resets the first byte of text to zero. Sets VARTAB to TXTTAB+2 and then. . .

RUNC $A659–$A65D : Resets execution to the start of the program (STXPTR) and then goes to CLEARC.

CLEAR $A65E–$A65F : CLR enters here. Checks syntax and then. . .

CLEARC $A660–$A676 : Sets FRETOP to MEMSIZ. Aborts I/O and sets ARYTAB to VARTAB and then. . .

LDCLR $A677–$A68D : Does RESTOR. Resets TEMPPT. Resets the stack.

STXPT $A68E–$A69B : Sets TXTPTR to TXTTAB-1 to reset execution to the start of the program.

LIST $A69C–$A716 : Entry point for the LIST command.

QPLOP $A717–$A741 : Handles the LIST character. If non-token (<128) or token in quotes, then print it. Otherwise expand the token and print it.

139

FOR $A742–$A7AD	: Entry point for the FOR command. Stores TXTPTR, CURLIN and the final value on the stack, and then. . .
NEWSTT $A7AE–$A7C3	: Checks for the STOP key, then handles the next BASIC statement from text.
CKEOL $A7C4–$A7E0	: Checks that the end of the line is also the end of the text. Otherwise, gives the next line parameters.
GONE $A7E1–$A7EC	: Executes a statement within a line.
GONE3 $A7ED–$A81C	: Enter a BASIC command and execute it.
RESTOR $A81D–$A82B	: Entry point for the RESTORE command. Resets DATPTR to the start of BASIC.
STOP $A82C–$A82E	: Entry point for the STOP command. Clears the carry (for the 'BREAK' message') and then jumps to the END routine.
END $A82F–$A833	: Entry point for the END command. Sets the carry and then. . .
FINID $A834–$A840	: If not in direct mode, then stores TXTPTR in OLDTXT and then. . .
STPEND $A841–$A856	: Stores CURLIN in OLDLIN and exits to READY (if carry set: END) or ERRFIN (if carry clear: STOP).
CONT $A857–$A870	: Entry point for the CONT command. Restores TXTPTR and CURLIN unless OLDTXT is zero, then prints the 'CAN'T CONTINUE' error message.
RUN $A871–$A882	: Entry point for the RUN command. Does CLR then GOTO.

GOSUB $A883–$A89F	: Entry point for the GOSUB command. Stores TXTPTR, CURLIN and GOSUB flag ($8D) on the stack, then GOTO.
GOTO $A8A0–$A8A2	: Entry point for the GOTO command. Reads a number from BASIC text into LINNUM and then. . .
GOTOC $A8A3–$A8D1	: Scans for the end of the current line. Searches for the LINNUM line and sets TXTPRT when found.
RETURN $A8D2–$A8D3	: Entry point for the RETURN command. Checks the syntax and then. . .
RTC $A8D4–$AF7	: Clears the stack up to the first GOSUB entry. Then sets TXTPRT and CURLIN from the stack.
DATA $A8F8–$A905	: Entry point for the DATA command. Scans the text for an end of statement. Updates TXTPRT to ignore.
DATAN $A906–$A90A	: Sets a scan for a statement delimitor (colon for zero byte) and then carries out a search. . .
SERCHX $A90B–$A92A	: Searches the text for a value in X or zero byte. Exit with Y set to the number of bytes to delimitor.
IF $A92B–$A93A	: Entry point for the IF command. Evaluates the expression, performs a REM if zero (FALSE).
REM $A93B–$A93F	: Entry point for the REM command. Scans for a zero byte and increments TXTPTR.
DOCOND $A940–$A94A	: If the condition is not zero (TRUE) then carries out the command or GOTO as appropriate.

ONGOTO $A94B–$A96A : Entry point for the ON command. Gets a number from the text and scans for a line number. Carries out a GOTO or GOSUB.

LINGET $A96B–$A9A4 : Reads an integer from text into LINNUM. An error will result if the value is not in the range zero to 63999.

LET $A9A5–$A9C3 : Entry point for the LET command. Finds the target variable in the variable space and sets FORPNT to point at it. Evaluates the expression then goes to PUTINT, PTFLPT, PUTTIM or GETSPT as appropriate.

PTFLPT $A9C4–$A9D5 : Puts FAC into the variable pointed to by FORPNT.

PUTINT $A9D6–$A9E2 : Puts the integer in FAC+3 into the variable pointed to by FORPNT.

PUTTIM $A9E3–$AA2B : Sets TI$ from a string. Sets INDEX1 to point the string and A to six (string length).

GETSPT $AA2C–$AA7F : Puts the string descriptor pointed to by FAC+3 into the string variable pointed to by FORPNT.

PRINTN $AA80–$AA85 : Entry point for the PRINT# command. Carries out CMD then restores default I/O. (Unlisten IEEE if device number>3.)

CMD $AA86–$AA99 : Entry point for the CMD command. Sets CMD output device from table then calls PRINT.

STRDON $AA9A–$AA9F : PRINT routine. Prints a string and checks for the end of print statement.

PRINT $AAA0–$AAB7 : Entry point for the PRINT command. Identifies PRINT parameters (SPC, TAB, etc) and evaluates expressions.

VAROP $AAB8–$AABB : Output variable. If a number converts to a string, output string.

NUMDON $AABC–$AAD6 : PRINT routine. Prints numeric.

CRDO $AAD7–$AAE7 : OUTPUT CR/LF. If CHANNL >127 then output CR only.

COMPRT $AAE8–$AB1D : Prints tabs or spaces for comma delimitor.

STROUT $AB1E–$AB20 : Prints the string pointed to by A/Y (lo/hi) until the zero byte is found.

STRPRT $AB21–$AB23 : Prints the string pointed to by FAC+3 until the zero byte is found.

OUTSTR $AB24–$AB3A : Prints the string pointed to by INDEX1 of length A.

OUTSPC $AB3B–$AB3E : Prints a space. (Cursor right if to the screen.)

PRTSPC $AB3F–$AB41 : Prints a space always.

OUTSKP $AB42–$AB44 : Prints the cursor always.

OUTQST $AB45–$AB46 : Prints a question mark.

OUTDO $AB47–$AB4C : Prints the value in A.

TRMNOK $AB4D–$AB7A : Handles error messages for GET, INPUT and READ.

GET $AB7B–$ABA4 : Entry point for the GET command. Checks that it is not direct (illegal), identifies if it is GET# and gets one character.

INPUTN $ABA5–$ABBE : Entry point for the INPUT# command. Sets the input device. Inputs the unlisten IEEE if the device >3.

INPUT $ABBF–$ABE9 : Entry point for the INPUT command. Outputs a prompt message if any. Carries out the input.

BUFFUL $ABEA–$ABF8 : Reads the input. If BBUFF is zero (no input string) then skip.

QINLIN $ABF9–$AC05 : Prints a '?' and inputs data into the BBUFF buffer.

READ $AC06–$AC0C : Entry point for the READ command. Sets the READ flag ($98) in INPFLG. Sets X and Y (lo/hi) to BUF.

INPCON $AC0D–$AC0E : Entry point to READ for the INPUT command. Sets the INPUT flag ($00) in INPFLG. Sets X and Y (lo/hi) to BUF.

INPCO1 $AC0F–$AC34 : Entry point to READ for the GET command. Sets the GET flag ($40) in INPFLG. Sets X and Y to (lo/hi) BUF.

RDGET $AC35–$AC42 : Part of the READ routine which gets a byte.

RDINP $AC43–$ACB7 : Part of the READ routine which INPUTs. Uses RDGET.

DATLOP $ACB8–$ACFB : Part of the READ routine which reads DATA values. Uses RDGET.

EXINT $ACFC–$AD0B : ASCII string '?EXTRA IGNORED<CR>'. (<CR> is a carriage return.)

TRYAGN $AD0C–$AD1D : ASCII string '?REDO FROM START<CR>'.

NEXT $AD1E–$AD60 : Entry point for the NEXT command. Gets NEXT's variable and confirms that the corresponding FOR is on the stack. Calculates the next loop variable value.

DONEXT $AD61–$AD89 : If the loop counter is valid then sets CURLIN and TXTPTR from the stack and re-enters the FOR loop.

FRMNUM $AD8A–$AD8C : Evaluates a numeric expression from BASIC text. Enters FRMEVL, then enters CHKNUM.

CHKNUM $AD8D–$AD8E : Tests VALTYP for a numeric result from FRMEVL. Exits to READY with 'TYPE MISMATCH ERROR' if a string is found.

CHKSTR $AD8F–$AF9D : Tests VALTYP for string result from FRMEVL. Exits to READY with 'TYPE MISMATCH ERROR' if a numeric is found.

FRMEVL $AF9E–$AE82 : Inputs and evaluates any expression in BASIC text. Sets VALTYP ($00 if numeric), $FF if string) and INTFLG ($00 if floating point, $80 if integer). If the expression is a numeric floating point, the result is returned in FAC. If the expression is a numeric integer then the result is returned in FAC+3 in hi/lo format. If the expression is a string, then a pointer to the string descriptor is returned in FAC+3 (this is usually a copy of VARPNT). If the expression is a variable, then VARNAM will be set to point to the first byte of the name. If an error is found in the expression, then the routine exists to READY with 'SYNTAX ERROR'.

EVAL $AE83–$AEA7 : Evaluates a single term in an expression. Identifies functions PI, TI, TI$, etc.

PIVAL $AEA8–$AEAC : Floating point value of PI (3.1415965).

QDOT $AEAD–$AEF0 : Evaluates the non-variable term in an expression.

PARCHK $AEF1–$AEF6 : Evaluates the expression within parenthesis in an expression.

CHKCLS $AEF7–$AEF9 : Checks that the character pointed to by TXTPTR is a right parenthesis. If not, print 'SYNTAX ERROR'.

CHKOPN $AEFA–$AEFC : Checks that the character pointed to by TXTPTR is a left parenthesis. If not, print 'SYNTAX ERROR'.

CHKCOM $AEFD–$AEFE : Checks that the character pointed to by TXTPTR is a comma. If not, print 'SYNTAX ERROR'.

SYNCHR $AEFF–$AF07 : Checks that the character pointed to by TXTPTR is the same as in the Accumulator. If not, print 'SYNTAX ERROR'.

SYNERR·$AF08–$AF0C : Prints the error message 'SYNTAX ERROR' and returns to BASIC.

DOMIN $AF0D–$AF13 : Creates a monadic minus or NOT for use in evaluation.

RSVVAR $AF14–$AF27 : Sets the carry if the variable pointed to by FAC+3 is a reserved variable (ST,TI,TI$).

ISVAR $AF28–$AF47 : Finds a variable named in the BASIC text. Sets VARNAM to point to the name in tables if found. Places numeric values in FAC and the string pointer in FAC+3.

TISASC $AF48–$AFA6 : Converts TI to an ASCII string and sets FAC+3 to point to the string.

ISFUN $AFA7–$AFB0 : Evaluates a function. Returns a numeric value in FAC and the string value as a pointer in FAC+3.

STRFUN $AFB1–$AFD0 : Stores the string descriptor of a string function on the stack and evaluates it.

146

NUMFUN $AFD1–$AFE5 : Evaluates the argument of a numeric function and calculates the function value.

OROP $AFE6–$AFE8 : Performs an OR command. Sets the OR flag and uses ANDOP to evaluate it.

ANDOP $AFE9–$B015 : Performs an AND command and then converts floating point values to a fixed point. Carries out an AND (or OR if the OR flag is set) and then converts it back to floating point.

DOREL $B016–$B01A : Performs the mathematical relations '<>' or '=' if a numeric expression uses NUMREL or if a string expression uses STRREL.

NUMREL $B01B–$B02D : Performs a numeric comparison.

STRREL $B02E–$B080 : Performs a string comparison.

DIM $B081–$B08A : Performs a DIM.

PTRGET $B08B–$B0E6 : Identifies a variable named in the BASIC text and places the name, not the pointer, to the name in VARNAM.

ORDVAR $B0E7–$B112 : Finds the variable whose name is in VARNAM and sets VARPNT to point to it. If necessary, uses NOTFNS to create a new variable.

ISLETC $B113–$B11C : Sets the carry if the character in the Accumulator is a letter.

NOTFNS $B11D–$B127 : Creates a new variable with a name (as in VARNAM) unless PTRGET is called by ISVAR.

NOTEVL $B128–$B193 : Creates a new variable with a name (as in VARNAM) and sets VARPNT to point to it.

FMAPTR $B194–$B1A4 : Sets ARYPNT to the start of an array and places a number of array dimensions in COUNT.

N32768 $B1A5–$B1A9 : Floating point value of 32768 in FLPT format.

FACINX $B1AA–$B1B1 : Converts FAC to an integer in A/Y (lo/hi).

INTIDX $B1B2–$B1BE : Evaluates an expression in the BASIC text as an integer in the range −32768 to +32767.

AYINT $B1BF–$B1D0 : Evaluates an expression in the BASIC text as an integer in the range zero to +32767.

ISARY $B1D1–$B217 : Gets the array parameters from the BASIC text and pushes them on the stack.

FNDARY $B218–$B260 : Finds an array whose name is found in VARNAM. Parameters read by ISARY.

IQERR $B248–B24C : Prints 'ILLEGAL QUANTITY' error and returns to BASIC.

NOTFDD $B261–$B30D : Creates an array from parameters on the stack.

INLPN2 $B30E–$B34B : Sets VARPNT to point at an element within an array.

UMULT $B34C–$B37C : Calculates the number of bytes in subscript Y of an array starting at VARPNT.

FRE $B37D–$B390 : Entry point for the FRE function. Carries out garbage collection and sets the function value to FRETOP-STREND.

CIVAYF $BC91–$B39D : Converts an integer in A and Y (lo/hi) to a floating point in FAC within the range zero to 32767.

POS $B39E–$B3A1 : Entry point for the POS function. Returns the value of CPOS in FAC.

SNGFT $B3A2–$B3A5 : Converts Y to floating point format in FAC within the range zero to 255.

ERRDIR $B3A6–$B3B2 : Prints 'ILLEGAL DIRECT' error if in direct mode, i.e. CURLIN = $FF.

DEF $B3B3–$B3E0 : Entry point for the DEF function. Creates the FN function.

GETFNM $B3E1–$B3F3 : Checks the syntax of FN, locates the FN descriptor and sets DEFPNT to point to it.

FNDOER $B3F4–$B422 : Entry point for the FN function. Gets the FN descriptor and then. . .

SETFNV $B423–$B464 : Puts TXTPTR onto the stack. Sets TXTPTR to start at FN in text, evaluates the expression and then resets TXTPTR from the stack.

STRD $B465–$B474 : Entry point for the STR$ function. Evaluates the expression and converts to an ASCII string.

STRINI $B475–$B486 : Creates space for a string whose descriptor is in FAC+3 and length in A. Exits with a new descriptor in DSCTMP and a pointer to an old descriptor in DSCPNT.

STRLIT $B487–$B4D4 : Scans the string starting at the location held in A and Y (lo/hi), and creates a descriptor. Exits with FAC+3 pointing to the descriptor. The string is expected to end with a null byte or '"'.

PUTNW1 $B4D5–$B4F3 : Sets the descriptor on the descriptor stack and updates the pointer.

GETSPA $B4F4–$B525 : Sets FRETOP and FRESPC for a new string whose length is in A.

GARBA2 $B526–$B5BC : Carries out garbage collection. Closes up the space in a string (space used by discarded strings).

DVARS $B58D–$B605 : Searches the variable and array tables for the next string descriptor to be saved by garbage collection.

GRBPAS $B606–$B63C : Moves a string up to overwrite unwanted strings in garbage collection.

CAT $B63D–$B679 : Concatenates two strings in an expression, then continues to evaluate the expression.

MOVINS $B67A–$B6A2 : Transfers a string whose descriptor is pointed to by STRNG1.

FRESTR $B6A3–$B6DA : Confirms string mode then performs string housekeeping (discard unwanted string). Enters with a pointer to the string descriptor in FAC+3 and exits with length in A and INDEX1 pointing to the start of the string.

FRETMS $B6DB–$B6EB : Updates the string descriptor stack pointer.

CHRD $B6EC–$B6FF : Entry point for the CHR$ function.

LEFTD $B700–$B72B : Entry point for the LEFT$ function.

RIGHTD $B72C–$B736 : Entry point for the RIGHT$ function.

MIDD $B737–$B760 : Entry point for the MID$ function.

PREAM $B761–$B77B : Pulls from the stack string descriptor pointer and stores it in DSCPNT. Pulls the string parameter to A.

LEN $B77C–$B781 : Entry point for the LEN function.

150

LEN1 $B782–$B78A	: Carries out string housekeeping, then forces numeric mode. Exits with string length in Y.
ASC $B78B–$B79A	: Entry point for the ASC function. Gets the first character in the string and converts it to floating point format.
GTBYTC $B79B–$B7AC	: Evaluates an expression in the BASIC text. Validates that the answer is in the range zero to 255, otherwise prints 'ILLEGAL QUANTITY' error. Returns the value in X.
VAL $B7AD–$B7B4	: Entry point for the VAL function. Confirms that the argument is a string and then . . .
STRVAL $B7B5–$B7EA	: Converts the string starting at INDEX1 of length A to a floating point value in FAC.
GETNUM $B7EB–$B7F6	: Reads parameters from the BASIC text for POKE or WAIT. Puts the first integer into INDEX1 and the second integer into INDEX2.
GETADR $B7F7–$B80C	: Converts FAC to an integer in INDEX1 in the range zero to 65535.
PEEK $B80D–$B823	: Entry point for the PEEK command.
POKE $B824–$B82C	: Entry point for the POKE command.
WAIT $B82D–$B848	: Entry point for the WAIT command.
FADDH $B849–$884F	: Add 0.5 to the value in FAC.
FSUB $B850–$B852	: Floating point subtraction . . . FAC=MFLPT at A/Y – FAC.
FSUBT $B853–$B861	: Entry point for subtraction . . . FAC=argument-FAC.
FADD5 $B862–$B866	: Part of the 'addition normalisation' routine.

FADD $B867–$B869	: Floating point addition . . . FAC = MFLPT at A/Y + FAC.
FADDT $B86A–$B97D	: Entry point for addition . . . FAC = argument + FAC.
OVERR $B97E–$B983	: Prints the 'OVERFLOW ERROR' message and return to BASIC.
MULSHF $B984–$B9BB	: Multiply by a byte.
FONE $B9BC–$B9C0	: Constant '1.0' in floating point format.
FVAROS $B9C1–$B9E9	: Various constants used for series evaluation of functions.
LOG $B9EA–$BA27	: Performs the LOG function. Checks that the argument is positive, then carries out a series evaluation of the function.
PMULT $BA28–$BA2F	: Multiplies FAC by the floating point number pointed to by A/Y (lo/hi) and puts the result in FAC.
PMULTT $BA30–$BA58	: Performs the 'floating point multiply' routine. Multiplies FAC by AFAC and the answer is placed in FAC.
MLTPLY $BA59–$BA8B	: Multiplies FAC by a byte and places the answer in RESHO.
CONUPK $BA8C–$BAB6	: Loads AFAC with the floating point value pointed to by A/Y (lo-hi).
MULDIV $BAB7–$BAD3	: Multiplication subroutine to test FAC and AFAC for underflow or overflow.
MLDVEX $BAD4–$BAE1	: If there is an overflow, prints the 'OVERFLOW ERROR' message. If there's an underflow then FAC is zeroed.
MUL10 $BAE2–$BAF8	: Multiplies FAC by 10 and puts the answer in FAC.
TENC $BAF9–$BAFD	: Constant '10.0' in floating point format.

DIV10 $BAFE–$BB06 : Divides FAC by 10 and places the answer in FAC.

FDIVF $BB07–$BB0E : Divides AFAC by the floating point number pointed to by A/Y (lo-hi) (sign in X) and puts the answer in FAC.

FDIV $BB0F–$BB11 : Divides AFAC by the floating point value pointed to by A/Y (lo-hi) and puts the answer in FAC.

FDIVT $BB12–$BBA1 : Performs floating point division routine . . . AFAC is divided by FAC and the answer is placed in FAC. On entry, A = FACEXP.

MOVFM $BBA2–$BBC6 : Loads FAC with the floating point number pointed to by A/Y (lo-hi).

MOV2F $BBC7–$BBC9 : Stores FAC in TEMPF2.

MOV1F $BBCA–$BBCF : Stores FAC in TEMPF1.

MOVXF $BBD0–$BBD3 : Stores FAC in the location pointed to by FORPNT.

MOVMF $BBD4–$BBFB : Stores FAC in the location pointed to by X/Y (lo-hi).

MOVFA $BBFC–BC0B : Loads FAC from AFAC.

MOVAF $BC0C–$BC1A : Loads AFAC from FAC.

ROUND $BC1B–$BC2A : Rounds off FAC.

SIGN $BC2B–$BC38 : Finds the sign of FAC and places the result in A. ($01 = positive, $00 = zero and $FF = negative.)

SGN $BC39–$BC3B : Performs the SGN function.

ACTOFC $BC3C–$BC43 : Stores A in FAC.

INTOFC $BC44–$BC57 : Stores the integer in FAC+1 as a floating point number in FAC. On entry, X should contain $90.

ABS $BC58–$BC5A : Performs the ABS function.

PCOMP $BC5B–$BC9A : Compares FAC with the floating point number pointed to by A/Y (lo-hi). The result is returned in A. ($01 means that FAC > by floating point number, $00 = equal to and $FF = FAC is less than the floating point number.)

QINT $BC9B–$BCCB : Converts the floating point number in FAC to a four byte integer in FAC+1 in hi-lo form.

INT $BCCC–$BCF2 : Performs the INT function . . . converts FAC to a four byte integer in FAC+1, then converts it back to floating point in FAC.

FIN $BCF3–$BDB2 : Converts an ASCII string, pointed to by TXTPTR in the BASIC text, to floating point format in FAC.

FLCNST $BCB3–$BDC1 : Floating point constants used in ASCII string conversion.

INPRT $BDC2–$BDCC : Prints 'IN', followed by the current line number in CURLIN.

LINPRT $BDCD–$BDD6 : Prints the current line number from CURLIN.

FACOUT $BDD7–$BDDC : Prints FAC as an ASCII string.

FOUT $BDDD–$BDDE : Converts FAC to an ASCII string starting at STACK and ending with a null byte. Note this routine corrupts $FF, which would otherwise have been a spare zero page location.

FYOUT $BDDF–$BE67 : Converts FAC to an ASCII string starting at STACK−1+Y.

FOUTIM $BE68–$BF10 : Converts TI to an ASCII string starting at STACK and ending with a null byte.

ASCIFT $BF11–$BF70 : Floating point constants used in ASCII conversion.

SQR $BF71–$BF7A : Performs the SQR function.

FPWRT $BF7B–$BFB3   : Performs exponation (raise to the power of)—AFAC to the power of FAC, and places the answer in FAC.

NEGOP $BFB4–$BFBE   : Negates FAC and places the answer in FAC.

EXPCNT $BFBF–$BFEC   : Floating point constants for the EXP function.

EXP $BFED–$BFFF   : Evaluates the EXP function.

THE OPERATING SYSTEM ROM

EXPCNT $E000–$E042 : Final part of the EXP function (continued from the BASIC ROM).

POLYX $E043–$E08C : Evaluates series for functions. On entry, A/Y (lo-hi) points to a single byte integer which is one less than the number of constants which follow. Converts the argument to the range zero to 0.999999999.

RNDCST $E08D–$E096 : Floating point constants for the RND evaluation.

RND $E097–$E0F8 : Performs the RND evaluation.

BIOERR $E0F9–$E10B : Handles the INPUT/OUTPUT error within BASIC.

BCHOUT $E10C–$E111 : BASIC output character routine. Uses the 'KERNAL CHROUT' routine.

BCHIN $E112–$E117 : BASIC input character routine. Uses the 'KERNAL CHRIN' routine.

BCKOUT $E118–$E11D : BASIC open output channel routine. Uses the 'KERNAL CHKOUT' routine.

BCKIN $E11E–$E123 : BASIC open channel for input routine. Uses the 'KERNAL CHKIN' routine.

BGETIN $E124–$E129 : BASIC get character routine. Uses the 'KERNAL GETIN' routine.

156

SYS $E12A–$E155	: Performs the SYS function. Puts values from SYSA, SYSX, SYSY and SYSS (780–783) before entering the machine code routine. Puts the values from the registers back into the above routines on return to BASIC.
SAVET $E156–$E15E	: Performs the SAVE command. Fetch the parameters from the BASIC text before calling the 'KERNAL' routine (name, device, secondary address).
SAVER $E15F–$E164	: Saves RAM to a specified device by jumping to the 'KERNAL SAVE' routine.
VERFYT $E165–$E167	: Performs the VERIFY command. Fetches the parameters from the BASIC text before calling the 'KERNAL' routine.
LOADT $E168–$E174	: Performs the LOAD command. Fetches the parameters from the BASIC text before calling the 'KERNAL' routine.
LOADR $E175–$E1BD	: Loads RAM from a specified device by jumping to the 'KERNAL' routine.
OPENT $E1BE–$E1C0	: Performs the OPEN command. Fetches the parameters from the BASIC text before calling the 'KERNAL' routine.
OPENR $E1C1–$E1C6	: Opens a specified file by jumping to the 'KERNAL' routine.
CLOSET $E1C7–$E1C9	: Performs the CLOSE command. Fetches the parameters from the BASIC text before calling the 'KERNAL' routine.
CLOSER $E1CA–$E1D3	: Closes a specified file by jumping to the 'KERNAL' routine.

SLPARA $E1D4–$E1FF : Gets the parameters from the BASIC text for LOAD/SAVE/ VERIFY. Calls this routine before calling the 'KERNAL' routine.

COMBYT $E200–$E205 : If TXTPTR points to a comma, then it reads a byte from the BASIC text.

DEFLT $E206–$E20D : If the end of statement is found, goes to the 'stack calling' routine and exits with default parameters set.

CMMERR $E20E–$E218 : Verifies that TXTPTR pointing to comma is not followed by a colon or null byte. Prints the 'SYNTAX ERROR' message if it is followed by a colon or a null byte.

OCPARA $E219–$E263 : Fetches the parameters from the BASIC text for the OPEN and CLOSE routines and sets defaults.

COS $E264–$E26A : Evaluates the COS function. Add PI/2 to FAC and then . . .

SIN $E26B–$E2B3 : Evaluates the SIN function.

TAN $E2B4–$E2DF : Evaluates the TAN function by computing SIN/COS.

PI2 $E2E0–$E2E4 : Floating point constant for PI/2.

TWOPI $E2E5–$E2E9 : Floating point constant for PI*2.

FR4 $E2EA–$E2EE : Floating point constant for 0.25.

SINFLT $E2EF–$E30D : Floating point constants for the SIN function evaluation.

ATN $E30E–$E33D : Evaluates the ATN function.

ATNCNT $E33E–$E37A : Floating point constants for the ATN function evaluation.

158

BASSFT $E37B–$E393	: BASIC warm start routine called by BREAK if the BRK instruction is encountered or Stop/Restore pressed. Closes channels and restores default I/O. Resets the stack and exits through IERROR with X=$80.
INIT $E394–$E396	: Initialises BASIC on reset (cold start or SYS 64738), and then calls INITV to set the BASIC vectors in $0300 to $030b and then. . .
INITNV $E397–$E3A1	: Calls INITCZ to set up the BASIC variable in block zero of RAM. Calls INTMS and then exits to BASIC 'READY'.
INITAT $E3A2–$E3B9	: CHRGET routine master copy. Copied down to page zero by INITCZ.
RNDSED $E3BA–$E3BE	: Floating point constant 0.811635157, used as the initial seed for random number generation.
INITCZ $E3BF–$E446	: Initialises the BASIC RAM. Sets USRPOK, ADRAY1 and ADRAY2 and copies INITAT and RNDSED to CHRGET and RNDX. Sets TXXTAB and FRETOP to LORAM and HIRAM. Sets first byte in the BASIC text area to zero.
BVTRS $E447–$E452	: ROM copies of BASIC vectors.
INITV $E453–$E45F	: Copies BVTRS to RAM block zero.
WORDS $E460–$E472	: Text 'BYTES FREE'.
FREMES $E473–$E497	: Text '*** COMMODORE BASIC V2 ***'. And XXXXX BASIC bytes free.

IOBASK $E500–$E504 : Returns in A/Y (lo-hi) the address of 6526 Complex Interface Adaptor (CIA) chip used by the IRQ routines (and the keyboard routines). This is part of the 'IOBASE KERNAL' routine.

SCRNK $E505–$E509 : Returns the screen organisation. X contains columns and Y contains rows. Entry through 'SCREEN KERNAL' vector.

PLOTK $E50A–$E517 : Sets/returns the cursor position: screen row through X and columns through Y. Sets the cursor if the carry is clear. Returns the cursor position if the carry is set on entry. Entry through 'PLOT KERNAL' vector.

INITIO $E518–$E565 : Initialises the input/output. This routine is called by the 'IOBASE KERNAL' routine.

HOME $E566–$E56B : Home cursor and reset screen line link table.

PLOTR $E56C–$E599 : Moves the cursor to TBLX, PNTR.

PANIC $E59A–$E5A0 : Resets the default I/O, including VIC II chip registers.

DFLTIO $E5A0–$E5A7 : Resets the default I/O and then. . .

VICINT $E5A8–$E5B3 : Restores the default values of the 6567 (VIC II) chip registers.

KBGET $E5B4–$E5C9 : Gets the characters from the keyboard buffer. GETIN routine comes here if DFLTN is equal to zero.

KBINP $E5CA–$E631 : Inputs character (not GET). KSINP comes here if CRSW = 0.

KSINP $E632–$E639 : Inputs character from the keyboard or the screen. CHRIN comes here if DFLTN = 0.

SCINP $E63A–$E683   : Inputs character from the screen. KSINP comes here if CRSW = 3.

TGLQT $E684–$E690   : Toggle quote flag (QTSW). During input, stops tokenisation of keywords within quotes.

SCPUT $E691–$E715   : Prints A to the screen. Used by SCNPNT

SCNPNT $E716–$E8A0   : Prints a character to the screen. Interprets cursor controls, colour changes, case changes, etc.

CKDECL $E8A1–$E8B2   : Checks for decrement of the line counter.

CKINL $E8B3–$E8CA   : Checks for increment of the line counter.

CKCOLR $E8CB–$E8D9   : Checks the colour.

SCNTAB $E8DA–$E8E9   : Table used for decoding screen.

SCROLL $E8EA–$EA30   : Screen scrolling routines.

IRQK $EA31–$EA86   : The main IRQ handling routine. (CINV vector points here.)

SCNKYK $EA87–$EB78   : Keyboard scan routine. Checks for a key depression and places characters in the keyboard queue. This is the routine pointed to by the KERNAL vector, SCNKEY.

KBDTBL $EB79–$ED08   : Keyboard matrix tables. Used by SCNKEY to convert key depression to ASCII characters. Tables exist for the various shift modes.

TALKK $ED09–$ED0B   : ORs A to convert a device number to a TALK address for the IEEE bus and transmits this as a command. This is the 'KERNAL' routine pointed to by TALK.

LSTNK $ED0C–$EDB8 : ORs A to convert a device number to a LISTEN address for the IEEE bus and transmits this as a command. This is the 'KERNAL' routine pointed to by LISTEN.

SCNDK $EDB9–$EDC6 : Converts A and transmits it as a LISTEN secondary address on the IEEE bus. This is the 'KERNAL' routine called by SECOND.

TKSA $EDC7–$EDDC : Converts A and transmits it as a TALK secondary address on the IEEE bus. This is the 'KERNAL' routine called by TKSA.

CIOUTK $EDDD–$EDEE : Transmits a byte on to the IEEE bus. The character is buffered so that 'hand-shaking' can be carried out. This in the 'CIOUT KERNAL' routine.

UNTLKK $EDEF–$EDFD : Transmits an UNTALK command on the IEEE bus. This is the 'KERNAL' routine which is addressed by the UNTALK vector.

UNLSNK $EDFE–$EE12 : Transmits an UNLISTEN command on the IEEE bus. The UNLSN vector comes here.

ACPTRK $EE13–$EEBA : A byte is 'hand-shaken' off the IEEE bus and placed in A. This is the 'ACPTR KERNAL' routine.

NMICNT $EEBB–$EF05 : Continuation of the main 'NMI interrupt' routine used for RS232 devices.

RSWRT $EF06–$EF58 : Outputs a byte to the RS232 channel 2.

RSBLD $EF59–$F0BC : Part of the 'NMI interrupt' routine which builds the individual bits, coming from the RS232 channel, into a byte.

KMSGTX $F0BD–$F12A : Text of the KERNAL error and control messages is stored here.

KMESSG $F12B–$F13D : Prints the KERNAL message to the screen.

GETINK $F13E–$F156 : Gets a character from the channel and returns it in A. If no character has been sent, then it returns a zero. This is the 'KERNAL GETIN' routine.

CHRINK $F157–$F1C9 : Inputs a character from the buffer into A. This is the 'KERNAL CHRIN' routine.

CHROTK $F1CA–$F20D : Outputs the byte in A to the output channel. This is the 'CHROUT KERNAL' routine.

CHKINK $F20E–$F24F : Allocates the file specified by X as the input channel. This is the routine used by the 'CHKIN KERNAL' routine.

CKOUTK $F250–$F290 : Allocates the file specified by X as the output channel. This is the routine used by the 'CHKOUT KERNAL' routine.

CLOSEK $F291–$F32E : A specifies the file to be closed. The details are removed from the device tables (LAT, FAT and SAT). Output files are tidied up. This is the 'CLOSE KERNAL' routine.

CLALLK $F32F–$F332 : This routine aborts all current I/O. The number of open files (contained in LNTND) is set to zero and any IEEE files are UNTALKed or UNLISTENed. The routine does not close 'output' files properly so may only be safely used with input (use CLOSE for output files). This is the 'CLALL KERNAL' routine.

163

CLRCHK $F333–$F349   : De-allocates the input/output channels and restores the default devices (DFLTN = 0 and DFLTO = 3). This is the 'KERNAL CLRCHN' routine.

OPENK $F34A–$F49D   : Opens the file whose specification is stored in FNLEN, LA, FA, SA and FNADR, by inserting the details in the LAT, FAT and SAT tables and carrying out the appropriate procedures for files on tape or disk. This is the 'KERNAL OPEN' routine.

LOADK $F49E–$F5DC   : Loads the file specified in FLEN, LA, FA, SA and FNADR, and the argument which specifies whether the file is to be re-loaded from whence it was saved or relocated elsewhere. This is the 'KERNAL LOAD' routine.

SAVEK $F5D–$F69A   : Saves the specified RAM (STAL and MEMUSS) onto the specified file (FNLEN, LA, FA, SA and FNADR). This is the 'KERNAL SAVE' routine.

UDTIMK $F69B–$F6EC   : Part of the IRQ interrupt which updates the real time jiffy clock. It also stores the current keyboard matrix value in STKEY, which enables STOP to function. This is the 'UDTIM KERNAL' routine.

STOPK $FE6D–$F6FA   : Checks the value stored in STKEY and returns with the Z flag set if the value stored represents the STOP key. This is the 'KERNAL STOP' routine.

KERROR $F6FB–$F72B   : Errors detected by the 'KER-NAL' routines enter this routine to output the appropriate error message.

THEADR $F72C–$F80C   : Finds and reads the header block on tape.

TCNTL $F80D–$F92B   : Tape control routines. These routines undertake functions such as switching cassette motors on and off, timing, etc.

TREAD $F92C–$FA6F   : Tape reading routines.

TBYT $FA70–$FBA5   : Byte handling routines for tape reading.

TWRT $FBA6–$FCE1   : Tape writing routines.

COLD $FCE2–$FE42   : Cold start routine. Normally accessed when the computer is initially switched on. It is the routine which is pointed to by the vector at $FFFC. Memory is initialised and all input/output devices are set up. The first part of the routine checks if a cartridge is plugged in by looking at the bytes from $FD10–$FD14. If the bytes are the same, then the routine jumps to the cartridge for initialisation. If these bytes are in RAM then the routine also jumps to the location specified to start. The jump addresses are stored as vectors: the start vector at $8000 and $8001; and the vector for when the Run/Stop key is pressed is at $8002 and $8003.

NMIXCT $FE43–$FF48   : NMI interrupt control.

INTRPT $FF48–$FF80   : This routine is entered when an interrupt occurs. Registers are saved and the source of the interrupt is determined—IRQ or BRK instruction. Appropriate actions are then taken.

165

KERNAL JUMP TABLE

As calling all the KERNAL routines is done by JSR command, I will only specify the start address of these routines.

CINT $FF81
: Initialises the screen editor and 6567 video chip. This routine should be the first routine called by a cartridge. To use, call this routine (JSR $FF81).

IOINIT $FF84
: This routine initialises all input/output devices. To use, call this routine.

RAMTAS $FF87
: This routine tests RAM and sets the top and bottom of memory pointers. It also clears locations $0000 to $0101 and $0200 to $033f. To use, call this routine.

RESTOR $FF8A
: This routine restores the default values of all vectors used by BASIC and the KERNAL. To use, call this routine.

VECTOR $FF8D
: This routine is used to change the values contained in the vectors. To read the vectors, set the carry. Load X and Y (lo-hi) with the address in memory where to put the vectors. Then change the ones that you want and clear the carry. Set X and Y to the address that the list is now located and call this routine to put the new list in the correct place in memory.

SETMSG $FF90
: This routine controls the printing of error messages. To use, load A with $40 to turn on control messages (eg. press play on tape); $80 to turn on error messages (eg. file not found); and $00 to turn off all messages.

SECOND $FF93
: Sends a secondary address to an I/O device. To use, load A with the secondary address to be sent and call this routine.

TKSA $FF96 : Sends a secondary address after TALK. To use, call the 'TALK' routine and then load A with the secondary address, and call this routine.

MEMTOP $FF99 : This routine reads/sets the top of memory. To read the top of memory, call this routine with the carry bit set. The top of memory will be loaded in the X and Y registers in lo-hi byte order. To set the top of memory clear the carry bit, and load X and Y with the top of memory in lo-hi byte order. Then call this routine.

MEMBOT $FF9C : This routine reads/sets the bottom of memory. To read the bottom of memory, call this routine with the carry bit set. The bottom of memory will be loaded in the X and Y registers in lo-hi byte order. To set the bottom of memory clear the carry bit, and load X and Y with the bottom of memory in lo-hi byte order. Then call this routine.

SCNKEY $FF9F : This routine reads the keyboard. If a key is held down then its ASCII value is placed in the keyboard buffer. To use, call this routine.

SETTMO $FFA2 : This routine sets the IEEE timeout. This routine is used *only* by an IEEE card. To use, load A with $00 and call this routine to set the timeout flag. To clear the timeout flag, load A with $80 and call this routine.

ACPTR $FFA5 : This routine gets a byte from the serial bus using full handshaking. To use, get the 'TALK' and 'TKSA KERNAL' routines to set a device to send data. Call this routine. Now store or do otherwise with the data.

CIOUT $FFA8 : Outputs a byte to the serial bus. To use, do LISTEN and SECOND, then load A with the byte to be sent. Now call this routine.

UNTLK $FFAB : This routine tells the devices on the serial bus to stop sending data. To use, call this routine.

UNLSN $FFAE : This routine tells the devices on the serial bus to stop receiving data. To use, call this routine.

LISTEN $FFB1 : This routine tells a device on the serial bus to prepare to receive data. To use, load A with the device number of the device that you want to listen to (0–31) and call this routine.

TALK $FFB4 : This routine tells a device on the serial bus to send data. To use this routine, load A with the device number of the device that you want to send data (0–31) and call this routine.

READST $FFB7 : This routine returns the current status of the I/O devices in A.

SETLFS $FFBA : This routine sets the logical file number, device address and the secondary address for other KERNAL routines. To use, load A with the logical file number, X with the device number (0 = keyboard, 1 = tape, 2 = RS232C, 3 = CRT display, 4/5 = serial bus printer, 8/9 = serial bus disk drive) and call this routine.

SETNAM $FFBD : This routine sets up the file name required for OPEN, SAVE and LOAD. To use, load A with the length of the file name, and X and Y with the address of the file name in lo-hi byte order. If no file name is required then load A with zero. Now call this routine.

OPEN $FFC0   : This routine is used to OPEN a logical file. To use, call SETLFS and SETNAM, and then call this routine.

CLOSE $FFC3   : This routine CLOSEs a logical file. To use, load A with the logical file to be closed and call this routine.

CHKIN $FFC6   : This routine opens a channel for input. To use, open the logical file with OPEN and load X with the number of the logical file to be used. Then call this routine.

CHKOUT $FFC9   : This routine opens a channel for output. To use, open the logical file with OPEN and load X with the logical file to be used. Then call this routine.

CLRCHN $FFCC   : This routine clears all open channels and restores the I/O channels to their original default values. To use, call this routine.

CHRIN $FFCF   : This routine gets a byte of data from an input channel. To use this routine, call OPEN and CHKIN, and then call this routine and store the data received in A.

CHROUT $FFD2   : This routine outputs a character to an already opened channel. To use, call OPEN and CHKOUT, and then call this routine with the byte to be output in A. If the characters are to be sent to the screen, then load A with the character and call this routine. No preparatory routines are required in this case.

LOAD $FFD5   : This routine loads or verifies RAM from a device. To load, A must be set to zero. To verify, A must be set to one. To use, call SETLFS and SETNAM, and then call this routine.

SAVE $FFD8 : This routine saves RAM to a device. To use, call SETLFS and SETNAM. Load two consecutive locations in zero page with the start address of the save in lo-hi byte format. Load A with the zero page offset of the save start address (if the save address is stored in $FB and $FC, then load A with $FB). Load X and Y with the end address +1 of the save in lo-hi byte format and call this routine.

SETTIM $FFDB : This routine sets the system clock. The clock is three bytes long and is stored as 'jiffies' (60ths of a second). To set the clock, load A with the most significant byte of the time, load X with the middle byte and load Y with the least significant byte. Then call this routine.

RDTIM $FFDE : This routine reads the system clock. To use, call this routine. A contains the most significant byte, X contains the next most significant byte and Y contains the least significant byte when the routine returns.

STOP $FFE1 : This routine checks if the Stop key is pressed. To use, call UDTIM, and then call this routine and test for the zero flag. If the flag is set then the Stop key was set.

GETIN $FFE4 : This routine gets a character from the keyboard buffer. To use, call this routine. If A contains zero then the buffer is empty, otherwise the data for the key pressed can be used.

CLALL $FFE7 : This routine closes all open files. To use, call this routine.

UDTIM $FFEA : This routine updates the system clock. It is called by the normal 'IRQ' routine every 60th of a second. To use, if you are using your own interrupt controller, call this routine.

SCREEN $FFED : This routine returns the format of the screen, ie. 40 in X and 25 in Y. To use, call this routine.

PLOT $FFF0 : This routine reads or sets the current cursor position. To read the current cursor position, set the carry and call this routine. The X co-ordinate will be in X and the Y co-ordinate in Y. To set the position of the cursor, clear the carry and load X with the X and Y with the Y. Then call this routine.

IOBASE $FFF3 : This routine defines the address of the memory section where the memory mapped I/O devices are located. To use this routine, call the routine and the X and Y registers will contain the address of the I/O start in memory in lo-hi byte format.

KVCTRS $FFFA–$FFFB : NMI vector address.

RSTVEC $FFFC–$FFFD : Reset vector address.

IRQVEC $FFFE–$FFFF : IRQ interrupt vector address.

APPENDICES

APPENDIX A

Here are all the necessary abbreviations for the BASIC keywords. You will find that most of the Commodore 64 BASIC keywords can be abbreviated when typing in programs. They are as follows:

Command	Abbreviation	Looks like this on screen	Command	Abbreviation	Looks like this on screen
ABS	A [SHIFT] B	A│	END	E [SHIFT] N	E╱
AND	A [SHIFT] N	A╱	EXP	E [SHIFT] X	E♣
ASC	A [SHIFT] S	A♥	FN	NONE	FN
ATN	A [SHIFT] T	A▏	FOR	F [SHIFT] O	F▔
CHR$	C [SHIFT] H	C▕	FRE	F [SHIFT] R	F▁
CLOSE	CL [SHIFT] O	CL▔	GET	G [SHIFT] E	G▔
CLR	C [SHIFT] L	C▁	GET#	NONE	GET#
CMD	C [SHIFT] M	C╲	GOSUB	GO [SHIFT] S	GO♥
CONT	C [SHIFT] O	C▔	GOTO	G [SHIFT] O	G▔
COS	NONE	COS	IF	NONE	IF
DATA	D [SHIFT] A	D♠	INPUT	NONE	INPUT
DEF	D [SHIFT] E	D▔	INPUT#	I [SHIFT] N	I╱
DIM	D [SHIFT] I	D╮	INT	NONE	INT

Com-mand	Abbrevi-ation	Looks like this on screen	Com-mand	Abbrevi-ation	Looks like this on screen
LEFT$	LE SHIFT F	LE ⊟	RIGHT$	R SHIFT I	R ◥
LEN	NONE	LEN	RND	R SHIFT N	R ◿
LET	L SHIFT E	L ⊓	RUN	R SHIFT U	R ◹
LIST	L SHIFT I	L ◥	SAVE	S SHIFT A	S ♠
LOAD	L SHIFT O	L ☐	SGN	S SHIFT G	S ◫
LOG	NONE	LOG	SIN	S SHIFT I	S ◥
MID$	M SHIFT I	M ◥	SPC(	S SHIFT P	S ☐
NEW	NONE	NEW	SQR	S SHIFT Q	S ●
NEXT	N SHIFT E	N ⊓	STATUS	ST	ST
NOT	N SHIFT O	N ☐	STEP	ST SHIFT E	ST ⊟
ON	NONE	ON	STOP	S SHIFT T	S ◫
OPEN	O SHIFT P	O ☐	STR$	ST SHIFT R	ST ⊟
OR	NONE	OR	SYS	S SHIFT Y	S ◫
PEEK	P SHIFT E	P ⊓	TAB(	T SHIFT A	T ♠
POKE	P SHIFT O	P ☐	TAN	NONE	TAN
POS	NONE	POS	THEN	T SHIFT H	T ◫
PRINT	?	?	TIME	TI	TI
PRINT#	P SHIFT R	P ▢	TIME$	TI$	TI$
READ	R SHIFT E	R ⊓	USR	U SHIFT S	U ♥
REM	NONE	REM	VAL	V SHIFT A	V ♠
RESTORE	RE SHIFT S	RE ♥	VERIFY	V SHIFT E	V ⊓
RETURN	RE SHIFT T	RE ◫	WAIT	W SHIFT A	W ♠

174

APPENDIX B

The following table contains the values for the screen display codes. (The values used for POKEing characters onto the screen and the values PEEKed from the screen.)

To change from character set 1 to set 2 and *vice versa*, press the Shift and Commodore keys simultaneously.

SCREEN CODES

SET 1	SET 2	POKE	SET 1	SET 2	POKE	SET 1	SET 2	POKE
@		0	C	c	3	F	f	6
A	a	1	D	d	4	G	g	7
B	b	2	E	e	5	H	h	8
I	i	9	%		37	♠	A	65
J	j	10	&		38	▯	B	66
K	k	11	'		39	▤	C	67
L	l	12	(		40	▢	D	68
M	m	13	)		41	▭	E	69
N	n	14	•		42	◻	F	70
O	o	15	+		43	◻	G	71
P	p	16	,		44	◻	H	72
Q	q	17	–		45	◰	I	73
R	r	18	.		46	◱	J	74
S	s	19	/		47	◲	K	75
T	t	20	0		48	◻	L	76
U	u	21	1		49	◺	M	77
V	v	22	2		50	◹	N	78
W	w	23	3		51	◻	O	79

SET 1	SET 2	POKE	SET 1	SET 2	POKE	SET 1	SET 2	POKE
X	x	24	4		52	(graphic)	P	80
Y	y	25	5		53	(graphic)	Q	81
Z	z	26	6		54	(graphic)	R	82
[		27	7		55	(graphic ♥)	S	83
£		28	8		56	(graphic)	T	84
]		29	9		57	(graphic)	U	85
↑		30			58	(graphic ⊠)	V	86
←		31	;		59	(graphic ◯)	W	87
SPACE		32	<		60	(graphic ♣)	X	88
!		33	=		61	(graphic)	Y	89
"		34	>		62	(graphic ♦)	Z	90
#		35	?		63	(graphic)		91
$		36	(graphic)		64	(graphic)		92
(graphic)		93	(graphic)	(graphic)	105	(graphic)		117
(graphic π)	(graphic)	94	(graphic)		106	(graphic)		118
(graphic)	(graphic)	95	(graphic)		107	(graphic)		119
SPACE		96	(graphic)		108	(graphic)		120
(graphic)		97	(graphic)		109	(graphic)		121
(graphic)		98	(graphic)		110	(graphic)	✓	122
(graphic)		99	(graphic)		111	(graphic)		123
(graphic)		100	(graphic)		112	(graphic)		124
(graphic)		101	(graphic)		113	(graphic)		125
(graphic)		102	(graphic)		114	(graphic)		126
(graphic)		103	(graphic)		115	(graphic)		127
(graphic)		104	(graphic)		116			

Codes from 128-255 are reversed images of codes 0-127.

APPENDIX C

The following table contains ASCII values for the characters and control codes. The values are those returned by the ASC function and the characters printed by the CHR$ function.

PRINTS	CHR$	PRINTS	CHR$	PRINTS	CHR$	PRINTS	CHR$
	0	CRSR ↓	17	"	34	3	51
	1	RVS ON	18	#	35	4	52
	2	CLR HOME	19	$	36	5	53
	3	INST DEL	20	%	37	6	54
	4		21	&	38	7	55
WHT	5		22	'	39	8	56
	6		23	(	40	9	57
	7		24	)	41		58
DISABLES SHIFT C=	8		25	*	42	;	59
ENABLES SHIFT C=	9		26	+	43	<	60
	10		27	,	44	=	61
	11	RED	28	–	45	>	62
	12	CRSR →	29	.	46	?	63
RETURN	13	GRN	30	/	47	@	64
SWITCH TO LOWER CASE	14	BLU	31	0	48	A	65
	15	SPACE	32	1	49	B	66
	16	!	33	2	50	C	67
D	68	♠	97	⊤	126	⊞	155
E	69	▯	98	◣	127	PUR	156
F	70	⊟	99		128	CMDR SHIFT	157
G	71	⊟	100	♠	129	YEL	158
H	72	▢	101		130	CYN	159
I	73	⊟	102		131	SPACE	160

PRINTS	CHR$	PRINTS	CHR$	PRINTS	CHR$	PRINTS	CHR$
J	74		103		132		161
K	75		104	f1	133		162
L	76		105	f3	134		163
M	77		106	f5	135		164
N	78		107	f7	136		165
O	79		108	f2	137		166
P	80		109	f4	138		167
Q	81		110	f6	139		168
R	82		111	f8	140		169
S	83		112	SHIFT RETURN	141		170
T	84		113	SWITCH TO UPPER CASE	142		171
U	85		114		143		172
V	86		115	BLK	144		173
W	87		116	CASH	145		174
X	88		117	RVS OFF	146		175
Y	89		118	CLR HOME	147		176
Z	90		119	INST DEL	148		177
[	91		120		149		178
£	92		121		150		179
]	93		122		151		180
↑	94		123		152		181
←	95		124		153		182
	96		125		154		183
	184		186		188		190
	185		187		189		191

CODES	192-223	SAME AS	96-127
CODES	224-254	SAME AS	160-190
CODE	255	SAME AS	126

APPENDIX D

The following diagrams contain the locations of character and colour RAM.

As an example, to put an 'A' in the top left of the screen in yellow, type the following:

POKE 1024,1
POKE 55296,7

The following charts list which memory locations control placing characters on the screen, and the locations used to change individual character colours, as well as showing character colour codes.

SCREEN MEMORY MAP

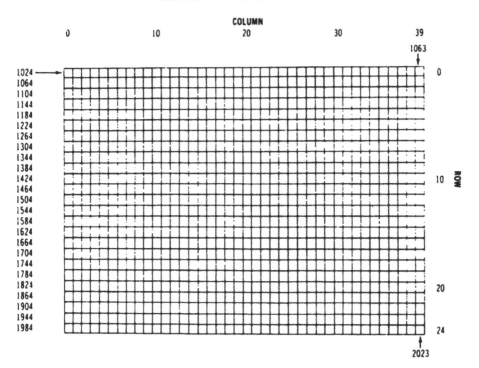

The actual values to POKE into a colour memory location to change a character's colour are:

0	BLACK	8	ORANGE
1	WHITE	9	BROWN
2	RED	10	Light RED
3	CYAN	11	GRAY 1
4	PURPLE	12	GRAY 2
5	GREEN	13	Light GREEN
6	BLUE	14	Light BLUE
7	YELLOW	15	GRAY 3

For example, to change the colour of a character located at the upper left-hand corner of the screen to red, type: POKE 55296,2.

COLOUR MEMORY MAP

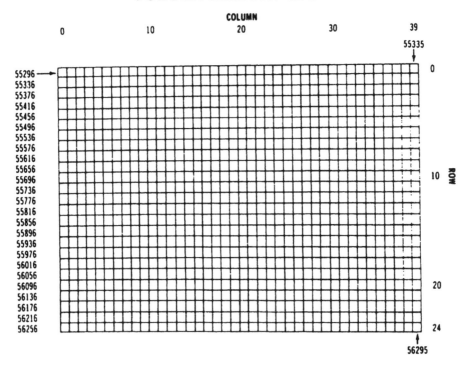

APPENDIX E

The following table contains the values for musical notes.
The table contains the note, octave, decimal value of the frequency, the hi-byte (to be POKEd into the hi-frequency registers) and the lo-byte (to be POKEd into the lo-frequency registers).

MUSICAL NOTE		OSCILLATOR FREQ		
NOTE	OCTAVE	DECIMAL	HI	LOW
0	C–0	268	1	12
1	C#–0	284	1	28
2	D–0	301	1	45
3	D#–0	318	1	62
4	E–0	337	1	81
5	F–0	358	1	102
6	F#–0	379	1	123
7	G–0	401	1	145
8	G#–0	425	1	169
9	A–0	451	1	195
10	A#–0	477	1	221
11	B–0	506	1	250
16	C–1	536	2	24
17	C#–1	568	2	56
18	D–1	602	2	90
19	D#–1	637	2	125
20	E–1	675	2	163
21	F–1	716	2	204
22	F#–1	758	2	246
23	G–1	803	3	35
24	G#–1	851	3	83
25	A–1	902	3	134
26	A#–1	955	3	187
27	B–1	1012	3	244
32	C–2	1072	4	48

MUSICAL NOTE		OSCILLATOR FREQ		
NOTE	OCTAVE	DECIMAL	HI	LOW
33	C#−2	1136	4	112
34	D−2	1204	4	180
35	D#−2	1275	4	251
36	E−2	1351	5	71
37	F−2	1432	5	152
38	F#−2	1517	5	237
39	G−2	1607	6	71
40	G#−2	1703	6	167
41	A−2	1804	7	12
42	A#−2	1911	7	119
43	B−2	2025	7	233
48	C−3	2145	8	97
49	C#−3	2273	8	225
50	D−3	2408	9	104
51	D#−3	2551	9	247
52	E−3	2703	10	143
53	F−3	2864	11	48
54	F#−3	3034	11	218
55	G−3	3215	12	143
56	G#−3	3406	13	78
57	A−3	3608	14	24
58	A#−3	3823	14	239
59	B−3	4050	15	210
64	C−4	4291	16	195
65	C#−4	4547	17	195
66	D−4	4817	18	209
67	D#−4	5103	19	239
68	E−4	5407	21	31
69	F−4	5728	22	96
70	F#−4	6069	23	181
71	G−4	6430	25	30
72	G#−4	6812	26	156
73	A−4	7217	28	49
74	A#−4	7647	29	223
75	B−4	8101	31	165
80	C−5	8583	33	135
81	C#−5	9094	35	134

MUSICAL NOTE		OSCILLATOR FREQ		
NOTE	OCTAVE	DECIMAL	HI	LOW
82	C-0	9634	37	162
83	C#-0	10207	39	223
84	D-0	10814	42	62
85	F-5	11457	44	193
86	F#-5	12139	47	107
87	G-5	12860	50	60
88	G#-5	13625	53	57
89	A-5	14435	56	99
90	A#-5	15294	59	190
91	B-5	16203	63	75
96	C-6	17167	67	15
97	C#-6	18188	71	12
98	D-6	19269	75	69
99	D#-6	20415	79	191
100	E-6	21629	84	125
101	F-6	22915	89	131
102	F#-6	24278	94	214
103	G-6	25721	100	121
104	G#-6	27251	106	115
105	A-6	28871	112	199
106	A#-6	30588	119	124
107	B-6	32407	126	151
112	C-7	34334	134	30
113	C#-7	36376	142	24
114	D-7	38539	150	139
115	D#-7	40830	159	126
116	E-7	43258	168	250
117	F-7	45830	179	6
118	F#-7	48556	189	172
119	G-7	51443	200	243
120	G#-7	54502	212	230
121	A-7	57743	225	143
122	A#-7	61176	238	248
123	B-7	64814	253	46

The following table lists the filter settings for the SID chip.

FILTER SETTINGS

Location	Contents
54293	Low cut-off frequency (0–7)
54294	High cut-off frequency (0–255)
54295	Resonance (bits 4–7) Filter voice 3 (bit 2) Filter voice 2 (bit 1) Filter voice 1 (bit 0)
54296	High pass (bit 6) Bandpass (bit 5) Low pass (bit 4) Volume (bits 0–3)

APPENDIX F

The following table contains a diagrammatic listing of the function of the VIC II chip and the individual bits.

Register # Dec	Hex	DB7	DB6	DB5	DB4	DB3	DB2	DB1	DB0	
0	0	S0X7							S0X0	SPRITE 0 X Component
1	1	S0Y7							S0Y0	SPRITE 0 Y Component
2	2	S1X7							S1X0	SPRITE 1 X
3	3	S1Y7							S1Y0	SPRITE 1 Y
4	4	S2X7							S2X0	SPRITE 2 X
5	5	S2Y7							S2Y0	SPRITE 2 Y
6	6	S3X7							S3X0	SPRITE 3 X
7	7	S3Y7							S3Y0	SPRITE 3 Y
8	8	S4X7							S4X0	SPRITE 4 X
9	9	S4Y7							S4Y0	SPRITE 4 Y
10	A	S5X7							S5X0	SPRITE 5 X
11	B	S5Y7							S5Y0	SPRITE 5 Y
12	C	S6X7							S6X0	SPRITE 6 X
13	D	S6Y7							S6Y0	SPRITE 6 Y
14	E	S7X7							S7X0	SPRITE 7 X Component
15	F	S7Y7							S7Y0	SPRITE 7 Y Component
16	10	S7X8	S6X8	S5X8	S4X8	S3X8	S2X8	S1X8	S0X8	MSB of X CO-ORD.
17	11	RC8	ECM	BMM	BLNK	RSEL	YSCL2	YSCL1	YSCL0	Y SCROLL MODE
18	12	RC7	RC6	RC5	RC4	RC3	RC2	RC1	RC0	RASTER
19	13	LPX7							LPX0	LIGHT PEN X
20	14	LPY7							LPY0	LIGHT PEN Y

Register # Dec	Hex	DB7	DB6	DB5	DB4	DB3	DB2	DB1	DB0	
21	15	SE7							SE0	SPRITE ENABLE (ON/OFF)
22	16	N.C.	N.C.	RST	MCM	CSEL	XSCL2	XSCL1	XSCL0	X SCROLL MODE
23 – 24	17	SEXY7							SEXY0	SPRITE EXPAND Y
24	18	VS13	VS12	VS11	VS10	CB13	CB12	CB11	N.C.	SCREEN Character Memory
25	19	IRQ	N.C.	N.C.	N.C.	LPIRQ	ISSC	ISBC	RIRQ	Interrupt Request's
26	1A	N.C.	N.C.	N.C.	N.C.	MLPI	MISSC	MISBC	MRIRQ	Interupt Request MASKS
27	1B	BSP7							BSP0	Background- Sprite PRIORITY
28	1C	SCM7							SCM0	MULTI- COLOUR SPRITE SELECT
29	1D	SEXX7							SEXX0	SPRITE EXPAND X
30	1E	SSC7							SSC0	Sprite- Sprite COLLISION
31	1F	SBC7							SBC0	Sprite- Background COLLISION

32	20	0	0	BLACK	EXT 1				EXTERIOR COL
33	21	1	1	WHITE	BKGD0				
34	22	2	2	RED	BKGD1				
35	23	3	3	CYAN	BKGD2				
36	24	4	4	PURPLE	BKGD3				
37	25	5	5	GREEN	SMC 0				SPRITE MULTICOLOUR 0
38	26	6	6	BLUE	SMC 1				1
39	27	7	7	YELLOW	S0COL				SPRITE 0 COLOUR
40	28	8	8	ORANGE	S1COL				1
41	29	9	9	BROWN	S2COL				2
42	2A	10	A	LT RED	S3COL				3
43	2B	11	B	GRAY 1	S4COL				4
44	2C	12	C	GRAY 2	S5COL				5
45	2D	13	D	LT GREEN	S6COL				6
46	2E	14	E	LT BLUE	S7COL				7
		15	F	GRAY 3					

LEGEND:
ONLY COLOURS 0–7 MAY BE USED IN MULTICOLOUR CHARACTER MODE

187

APPENDIX G

The following table contains the Commodore 64 BASIC equivalents of mathematical functions.

FUNCTION	BASIC EQUIVALENT
SECANT	SEC(X)=1/COS(X)
COSECANT	CSC(X)=1/SIN(X)
COTANGENT	COT(X)=1/TAN(X)
INVERSE SINE	ARCSIN(X)=ATN(X/SQR(−X*X+1))
INVERSE COSINE	ARCCOS(X)=−ATN(X/SQR (−X*X+1))+π/2
INVERSE SECANT	ARCSEC(X)=ATN(X/SQR(X*X−1))
INVERSE COSECANT	ARCCSC(X)=ATN(X/SQR(X*X−1)) +(SGN(X)−1*π/2
INVERSE COTANGENT	ARCOT(X)=ATN(X)+π/2
HYPERBOLIC SINE	SINH(X)=(EXP(X)−EXP(−X))/2
HYPERBOLIC COSINE	COSH(X)=(EXP(X)+EXP(−X))/2
HYPERBOLIC TANGENT	TANH(X)=EXP(−X)/(EXP(x)+EXP (−X))*2+1
HYPERBOLIC SECANT	SECH(X)=2/(EXP(X)+EXP(−X))
HYPERBOLIC COSECANT	CSCH(X)=2/(EXP(X)−EXP(−X))
HYPERBOLIC COTANGENT	COTH(X)=EXP(−X)/(EXP(X) −EXP(−X))*2+1
INVERSE HYPERBOLIC SINE	ARCSINH(X)=LOG(X+SQR(X*X+1))
INVERSE HYPERBOLIC COSINE	ARCCOSH(X)=LOG(X+SQR(X*X−1))
INVERSE HYPERBOLIC TANGENT	ARCTANH(X)=LOG((1+X)/(1−X))/2
INVERSE HYPERBOLIC SECANT	ARCSECH(X)=LOG((SQR (−X*X+1)+1/X)
INVERSE HYPERBOLIC COSECANT	ARCCSCH(X)=LOG((SGN(X)*SQR (X*X+1/x)
INVERSE HYPERBOLIC COTANGENT	ARCCOTH(X)=LOG((X+1)/(x−1))/2

APPENDIX H

The following pages contain the pin-out information for connecting external equipment to the Commodore 64.

1) Game I/0   4) Serial I/O (Disk/Printer)
2) Cartridge Slot   5) Modulator Output
3) Audio/Video   6) Cassette
                   7) User Port

Control Port 1

Pin	Type	Note
1	JOYA0	
2	JOYA1	
3	JOYA2	
4	JOYA3	
5	POT AY	
6	BUTTON A/LP	
7	+5V	MAX. 50mA
8	GND	
9	POT AX	

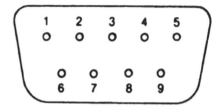

Control Port 2

Pin	Type	Note
1	JOYB0	
2	JOYB1	
3	JOYB2	
4	JOYB3	
5	POT BY	
6	BUTTON B	
7	+5V	MAX. 50mA
8	GND	
9	POT BX	

189

Cartridge Expansion Slot

Pin	Type
12	BA
13	$\overline{DMA}$
14	D7
15	D6
16	D5
17	D4
18	D3
19	D2
20	D1
21	D0
22	GND

Pin	Type
1	GND
2	+5V
3	+5V
4	$\overline{IRQ}$
5	$R/\overline{W}$
6	Dot Clock
7	I/O 1
8	$\overline{GAME}$
9	$\overline{EXROM}$
10	I/O 2
11	$\overline{ROML}$

Pin	Type
N	A9
P	A8
R	A7
S	A6
T	A5
U	A4
V	A3
W	A2
X	A1
Y	A0
Z	GND

Pin	Type
A	GND
B	$\overline{ROMH}$
C	$\overline{RESET}$
D	$\overline{NMI}$
E	S 02
F	A15
H	A14
J	A13
K	A12
L	A11
M	A10

```
22 21 20 19 18 17 16 15 14 13 12 11 10  9  8  7  6  5  4  3  2  1
■ ■ ■ ■ ■ ■ ■ ■ ■ ■ ■ ■ ■ ■ ■ ■ ■ ■ ■ ■ ■ ■

■ ■ ■ ■ ■ ■ ■ ■ ■ ■ ■ ■ ■ ■ ■ ■ ■ ■ ■ ■ ■ ■
 Z  Y  X  W  V  U  T  S  R  P  N  M  L  K  J  H  F  E  D  C  B  A
```

Audio/Video

Pin	Type	Note
1	LUMINANCE	
2	GND	
3	AUDIO OUT	
4	VIDEO OUT	
5	AUDIO IN	

Serial I/O

Pin	Type
1	SERIAL $\overline{SRQIN}$
2	GND
3	SERIAL ATN IN/OUT
4	SERIAL CLK IN/OUT
5	SERIAL DATA IN/OUT
6	$\overline{RESET}$

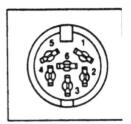

190

Cassette

Pin	Type
A-1	GND
B-2	+5V
C-3	CASSETTE MOTOR
D-4	CASSETTE READ
E-5	CASSETTE WRITE
F-6	CASSETTE SENSE

User I/O

Pin	Type	Note
1	GND	
2	+5V	MAX. 100 mA
3	$\overline{RESET}$	
4	CNT1	
5	SP1	
6	CNT2	
7	SP2	
8	$\overline{PC2}$	
9	SER. ATN IN	
10	9 VAC	MAX. 100 mA
11	9 VAC	MAX. 100 mA
12	GND	

Pin	Type	Note
A	$\overline{GND}$	
B	$\overline{FLAG2}$	
C	PB0	
D	PB1	
E	PB2	
F	PB3	
H	PB4	
J	PB5	
K	PB6	
L	PB7	
M	PA2	
N	GND	

191

APPENDIX I

The following pages list all the error messages generated by the Commodore 64 and the reason for them appearing.

BAD DATA   String data was received from an open file, but the program was expecting numeric data.

BAD SUBSCRIPT   The program was trying to reference an element of an array whose number is outside of the range specified in the DIM statement.

CAN'T CONTINUE   The CONT command will not work, either because the program was never RUN, there has been an error, or a line has been edited.

DEVICE NOT PRESENT   The required I/O device was not available for an OPEN, CLOSE, CMD, PRINT#, INPUT# or GET#.

DIVISION BY ZERO   Division by zero is a mathematical oddity and not allowed.

EXTRA IGNORED   Too many items of data were typed in response to an INPUT statement. Only the first few items were accepted.

FILE NOT FOUND   If you were looking for a file on tape, an END-OF-TAPE marker was found. If you were looking on disk, no file with that name exists.

FILE NOT OPEN   The file specified in a CLOSE, CMD, PRINT#, INPUT# or GET#, must first be OPENed.

FILE OPEN   An attempt was made to open a file using the number of an already open file.

FORMULA TOO COMPLEX   The string expression being evaluated should be split into at least two parts for the system to work with, or a formula has too many parentheses.

ILLEGAL DIRECT   The INPUT statement can only be used within a program, and not in direct mode.

ILLEGAL QUANTITY   A number used as the argument of a function or statement is out of the allowable range.

LOAD   There is a problem with the program on tape.

NEXT WITHOUT FOR   This is caused by either nesting

loops incorrectly or having a variable name in a NEXT statement that doesn't correspond with one in a FOR statement.

NOT INPUT FILE An attempt was made to INPUT or GET data from a file which was specified to be for output only.

NOT OUTPUT FILE An attempt was made to PRINT data to a file which was specified as input only.

OUT OF DATA A READ statement was executed but there is no data left unREAD in a DATA statement.

OUT OF MEMORY There is no more RAM available for program or variables. This may also occur when too many FOR loops have been nested, or when there are too many GOSUBs in effect.

OVERFLOW The result of a computation is larger than the largest number allowed, which is 1.70141884E+38.

REDIM'D ARRAY An array may only be DIMensioned once. If an array variable is used before that array is DIMd, an automatic DIM operation is performed on that array setting the number of elements to 10, and any subsequent DIMs will cause this error.

REDO FROM START Character data was typed in during an INPUT statement when numeric data was expected. Just re-type the entry so that it is correct, and the program will continue by itself.

RETURN WITHOUT GOSUB A RETURN statement was encountered, and no GOSUB command has been issued.

STRING TOO LONG A string can contain up to 255 characters.

?SYNTAX ERROR A statement is unrecognizable by the Commodore 64. A missing or extra parenthesis, misspelled keywords, etc.

TYPE MISMATCH This error occurs when a number is used in place of a string, or *vice versa*.

UNDEF'D FUNCTION A user-defined function was referenced, but it has never been defined using the DEF FN statement.

UNDEF'D STATEMENT An attempt was made to GOTO, GOSUB or RUN a line number that doesn't exist.

VERIFY The program on tape or disk does not match the program currently in memory.

APPENDIX J

6510 MICROPROCESSOR CHIP SPECIFICATIONS

DESCRIPTION

The 6510 is a low-cost microcomputer system capable of solving a broad range of small-systems and peripheral-control problems at minimum cost to the user.

An eight-bit bi-directional I/O port is located on-chip with the output register at address 0000 and the data-direction register at address 0001. The I/O port is bit-by-bit programmable.

The three-state 16-bit address bus allows Direct Memory Accessing (DMA) and multiprocessor systems sharing a common memory.

The internal processor architecture is identical to the MOS Technology 6502 to provide software compatibility.

FEATURES OF THE 6510 . . .

- Eight-bit bi-directional I/O port
- Single +5 volt supply
- N-channel, silicon gate, depletion load technology
- Eight-bit parallel processing
- 56 instructions
- Decimal and binary arithmetic
- Thirteen addressing modes
- True indexing capability
- Programmable stack pointer
- Variable length stack
- Interrupt capability
- Eight-bit bi-directional data bus
- Addressable memory range of up to 65K
- Direct memory access capability
- Bus compatible with M6800
- Pipeline architecture
- 1 MHz and 2 MHz operation
- Use with any type or speed memory

PIN CONFIGURATION

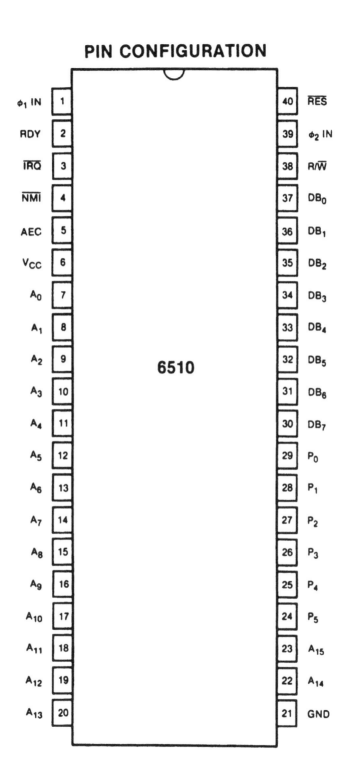

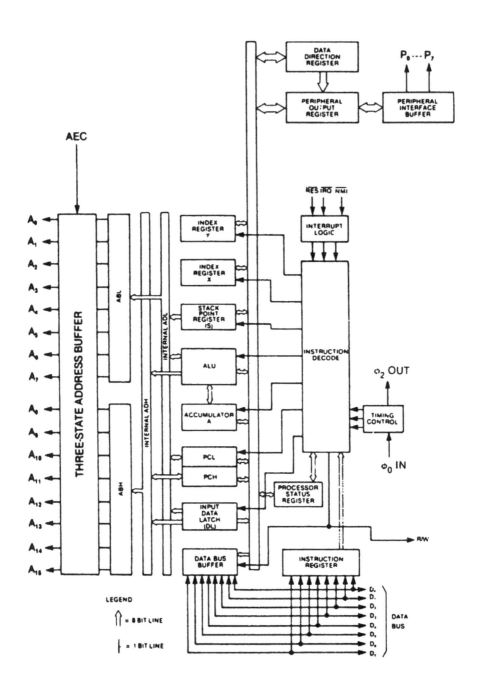

6510 BLOCK DIAGRAM

196

6510 CHARACTERISTICS

MAXIMUM RATINGS

RATING	SYMBOL	VALUE	UNIT
SUPPLY VOLTAGE	V_{CC}	−0.3 to +7.0	V_{DC}
INPUT VOLTAGE	V_{in}	−0.3 to +7.0	V_{DC}
OPERATING TEMPERATURE	T_A	0 to +70	°C
STORAGE TEMPERATURE	T_{STG}	−55 to +150	°C

NOTE: This device contains input protection against damage due to high static voltages or electric fields; however, precautions should be taken to avoid application of voltages higher than the maximum rating.

ELECTRICAL CHARACTERISTICS
(VCC = 5.0 V ±5%, VSS = 0, T_A = 0° to +70°C)

CHARACTERISTIC	SYM-BOL	MIN.	TYP.	MAX.	UNIT
Input High Voltage ϕ_1, $\phi_{2(in)}$	V_{IH}	$V_{CC} - 0.2$	—	$V_{CC} + 1.0V$	V_{DC}
Input High Voltage $\overline{RES}$, P_0-P_7 $\overline{IRQ}$, Data		$V_{SS} + 2.0$	—	—	V_{DC}
Input Low Voltage ϕ_1, $\phi_{2(in)}$	V_{IL}	$V_{SS} - 0.3$	—	$V_{SS} + 0.2$	V_{DC}
$\overline{RES}$, P_0-P_7 $\overline{IRQ}$, Data		—	—	$V_{SS} + 0.8$	V_{DC}
Input Leakage Current (V_{in} = 0 to 5.25V, V_{CC} = 5.25V) Logic	I_{in}	—	—	2.5	μA
ϕ_1, $\phi_{2(in)}$		—	—	100	μA
Three State (Off State) Input Current (V_{in} = 0.4 to 2.4V, V_{CC} = 5.25V) Data Lines	I_{TSI}	—	—	10	μA
Output High Voltage (I_{OH} = −100μA_{DC}, V_{CC} = 4.75V) Data, A0-A15, R/W, P_0-P_7	V_{OH}	$V_{SS} + 2.4$	—	—	V_{DC}

197

CHARACTERISTIC	SYM-BOL	MIN.	TYP.	MAX.	UNIT
Out Low Voltage ($I_{OL} = 1.6mA_{DC}$, $V_{CC} = 4.75V$) Data, A0-A15, R/W, P_0-P_7	V_{OL}	—	—	$V_{SS} + 0.4$	V_{DC}
Power Supply Current	I_{CC}	—	125		mA
Capacitance $V_{in} = 0$, $T_A = 25°C$, f = 1MHz)	C				pF
Logic, P_0-P_7	C_{in}	—	—	10	
Data		—	—	15	
A0-A15, R/W	C_{out}	—	—	12	
ϕ_1	$C\phi_1$	—	30	50	
ϕ_2	$C\phi_2$	—	50	80	

CLOCK TIMING

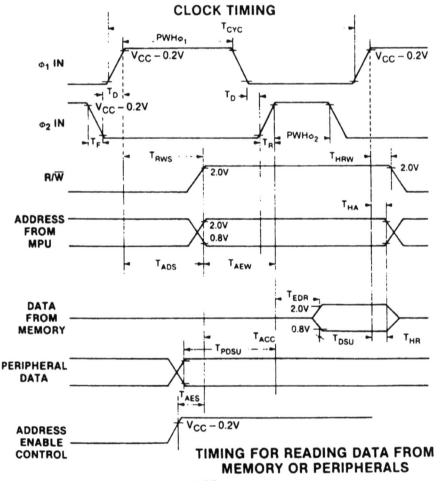

TIMING FOR READING DATA FROM MEMORY OR PERIPHERALS

CLOCK TIMING

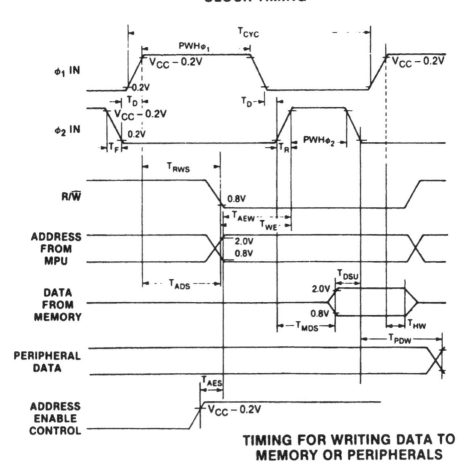

TIMING FOR WRITING DATA TO MEMORY OR PERIPHERALS

199

AC CHARACTERISTICS

ELECTRICAL CHARACTERISTICS (V_{CC} = 5 V ±5%, V_{SS} = 0 V, T_A = 0°–70°C)

CLOCK TIMING

CHARACTERISTIC	SYMBOL	1MHz TIMING			2 MHz TIMING			UNITS
		MIN.	TYP.	MAX.	MIN.	TYP.	MAX.	
Cycle Time	T_{CYC}	1000	—	—	500	—	—	ns
Clock Pulse Width φ1 (Measured at V_{cc}—0.2V) φ2	PWHφ1 PWHφ2	430 470	— —	— —	215 235	— —	— —	ns ns
Fall Time, Rise Time (Measured from 0.2V to V_{CC}—0.2V)	T_F, T_R	—	—	25	—	—	15	ns
Delay Time between Clocks (Measured at 0.2V)	T_D	0	—	—	0	—	—	ns

READ/WRITE TIMING (LOAD = 1TTL)

CHARACTERISTIC	SYMBOL	1 MHz TIMING			2 MHz TIMING			UNITS
		MIN.	TYP.	MAX.	MIN.	TYP.	MAX.	
Read/Write Set-up Time from 6508	T_{RWS}	—	100	300	—	100	150	ns
Address Set-up Time from 6508	T_{ADS}	—	100	300	—	100	150	ns
Memory Read Access Time	T_{ACC}	—	—	575	—	—	300	ns
Data Stability Time Period	T_{DSU}	100	—	—	50	—	—	ns

Characteristic	Symbol							Unit
Data Hold Time-Read	T_{HR}	—	—					ns
Data Hold Time-Write	T_{HW}	10	30	—	10	30		ns
Data Set-up Time from 6510	T_{MDS}	—	150	200	—	75	100	ns
Address Hold Time	T_{HA}	10	30	—	10	30		ns
R/W Hold Time	T_{HRW}	10	30	—	10	30		ns
Delay Time, Address valid to φ2 positive transition	T_{AEW}	180	—	—				ns
Delay Time, φ2 positive transition to Data valid on bus	T_{EDR}	—	—	395				ns
Delay Time, Data valid to φ2 negative transition	T_{DSU}	300	—	—				ns
Delay Time, R/W negative transition to φ2 positive transition	T_{WE}	130	—	—				ns
Delay Time, φ2 negative transition to Peripheral Data valid	T_{PDW}	—	—	1				µS
Peripheral Data Set-up Time	T_{PDSU}	300	—	—				ns
Address Enable Set-up Time	T_{AES}			60			60	ns

SIGNAL DESCRIPTION

Clocks (ϕ_1, ϕ_2)

The 6510 requires a two-phase non-overlapping clock that runs at the V_{CC} voltage level.

Address Bus (A_0–A_{15})

These outputs are TTL compatible, capable of driving one standard TTL load and 130 pf.

Data Bus (D_0–D_7)

Eight pins are used for the data bus. This is a bi-directional bus, transferring data to and from the device and peripherals. The outputs are tri-state buffers capable of driving one standard TTL load and 130 pf.

Reset

This input is used to reset or start the microprocessor from a power down condition. During the time that this line is held low, writing to or from the microprocessor is inhibited. When a positive edge is detected on the input, the microprocessor will immediately begin the reset sequence.

After a system initialisation time of six clock cycles, the mask interrupt flag will be set and the microprocessor will load the program counter from the memory vector locations FFFC and FFFD. This is the start location for program control.

After V_{CC} reaches 4.75 volts in a power-up routine, reset must be held low for at least two cycles. At this time the R/W signal will become valid.

When the reset signal goes high following these two clock cycles, the microprocessor will proceed with the normal reset procedure detailed above.

Interrupt Request (IRQ)

This TTL level input requests that an interrupt sequence begin within the microprocessor. The microprocessor will complete the current instruction being executed before recognising the request. At that time, the interrupt mask bit in the Status Code Register will be examined. If the interrupt mask flag is not set, the microprocessor will begin an interrupt sequence. The Program Counter and Processor Status Register are stored in the stack. The microprocessor will then set the interrupt mask flag high so that no further interrupts may occur. At the end of this cycle, the program counter low will be loaded from address FFFE, and program counter high from location FFFF, therefore transferring program control to the memory vector located at these addresses.

Address Enable Control (AEC)

The address bus is valid only when the 'address enable control' line is high. When low, the address bus is in a high-impedance state. This feature allows easy DMA and multiprocessor systems.

I/O Port (P_0–P_7)

Eight pins are used for the peripheral port, which can transfer data to or from peripheral devices. The output register is located in RAM at address 0001, and the data direction register is at address 0000. The outputs are capable at driving one standard TTL load and 130 pf.

Read/Write (R/W)

This signal is generated by the microprocessor to control the direction of data transfers on the data bus. This line is high except when the microprocessor is writing to memory or a peripheral device.

APPENDIX K

The following tables contain the timing values for the 6510 chip.

Each mode cell lists: OP (opcode), n (cycles), # (bytes). Condition Code columns: N Z C I D V.

Mnemonic	Operation	Immediate	Absolute	Zero Page	Accum.	Implied	(Ind.) X	(Ind.) Y	Z. Page, X	Abs. X	Abs. Y	Relative	Indirect	Z. Page, Y	Condition Code (N Z C I D V)
ADC	A + M + C → A (4)	69 2 2	6D 4 3	65 3 2			61 6 2	71 5 2	75 4 2	7D 4 3	79 4 3				✓ ✓ ✓ — — ✓
AND	A∧M → A (1)	29 2 2	2D 4 3	25 3 2			21 6 2	31 5 2	35 4 2	3D 4 3	39 4 3				✓ ✓ — — — —
ASL	C ← [7...0] ← 0		0E 6 3	06 5 2	0A 2 1				16 6 2	1E 7 3					✓ ✓ ✓ — — —
BCC	BRANCH ON C=0 (2)											90 2 2			— — — — — —
BCS	BRANCH ON C=1 (2)											B0 2 2			— — — — — —
BEQ	BRANCH ON Z=1 (2)											F0 2 2			— — — — — —
BIT	A∧M		2C 4 3	24 3 2											M_7 — — — — M_6
BMI	BRANCH ON N=1 (2)											30 2 2			— — — — — —
BNE	BRANCH ON Z=0 (2)											D0 2 2			— — — — — —
BPL	BRANCH ON N=0 (2)											10 2 2			— — — — — —
BRK	(See Fig. 1)					00 7 1									— — — 1 — —
BVC	BRANCH ON V=0 (2)											50 2 2			— — — — — —
BVS	BRANCH ON V=1 (2)											70 2 2			— — — — — —
CLC	0 → C					18 2 1									— — 0 — — —
CLD	0 → D					D8 2 1									— — — — 0 —
CLI	0 → I					58 2 1									— — — 0 — —
CLV	0 → V					B8 2 1									— — — — — 0
CMP	A - M (1)	C9 2 2	CD 4 3	C5 3 2			C1 6 2	D1 5 2	D5 4 2	DD 4 3	D9 4 3				✓ ✓ ✓ — — —
CPX	X - M	E0 2 2	EC 4 3	E4 3 2											✓ ✓ ✓ — — —
CPY	Y - M	C0 2 2	CC 4 3	C4 3 2											✓ ✓ ✓ — — —
DEC	M - 1 → M		CE 6 3	C6 5 2					D6 6 2	DE 7 3					✓ ✓ — — — —
DEX	X - 1 → X					CA 2 1									✓ ✓ — — — —
DEY	Y - 1 → Y					88 2 1									✓ ✓ — — — —
EOR	A⊻M → A (1)	49 2 2	4D 4 3	45 3 2			41 6 2	51 5 2	55 4 2	5D 4 3	59 4 3				✓ ✓ — — — —
INC	M + 1 → M		EE 6 3	E6 5 2					F6 6 2	FE 7 3					✓ ✓ — — — —
INX	X + 1 → X					E8 2 1									✓ ✓ — — — —
INY	Y + 1 → Y					C8 2 1									✓ ✓ — — — —
JMP	JUMP TO NEW LOC.		4C 3 3										6C 5 3		— — — — — —
JSR	(See Fig. 2) JUMP SUB		20 6 3												— — — — — —
LDA	M → A (1)	A9 2 2	AD 4 3	A5 3 2			A1 6 2	B1 5 2	B5 4 2	BD 4 3	B9 4 3				✓ ✓ — — — —

INSTRUCTIONS

Mnemonic	Operation	Immediate OP	N	#	Absolute OP	N	#	Zero Page OP	N	#	Accum. OP	N	#	Implied OP	N	#	(Ind,X) OP	N	#	(Ind),Y OP	N	#	Z.Page,X OP	N	#	Abs.X OP	N	#	Abs.Y OP	N	#	Relative OP	N	#	Indirect OP	N	#	Z.Page,Y OP	N	#	N	Z	C	I	D	V
LDX	M→X (1)	A2	2	2	AE	4	3	A6	3	2																	BE	4	3							B6	4	2	✓	✓	—	—	—	—
LDY	M→Y (1)	A0	2	2	AC	4	3	A4	3	2												BC	4	3													✓	✓	—	—	—	—
LSR	0→[7...0]→C				4E	6	3	46	5	2	4A	2										56	6	2	5E	7	3													0	✓	✓	—	—	—
NOP	NO OPERATION													EA	2	1																								—	—	—	—	—	—
ORA	AVM→A	09	2	2	0D	4	3	05	3	2							01	6	2	11	5	2	15	4	2	1D	4	3	19	4	3									✓	✓	—	—	—	—
PHA	A→Ms S-1→S													48	3	1																								—	—	—	—	—	—
PHP	P→Ms S-1→S													08	3	1																								—	—	—	—	—	—
PLA	S+1→S Ms→A													68	4	1																								✓	✓	—	—	—	—
PLP	S+1→S Ms→P													28	4	1																								(RESTORED)					
ROL	[7...0] with C				2E	6	3	26	5	2	2A	2										36	6	2	3E	7	3													✓	✓	✓	—	—	—
ROR	[7...0] with C				6E	6	3	66	5	2	6A	2										76	6	2	7E	7	3													(RESTORED)					
RTI	(See Fig. 1) RTRN INT													40	6	1																								(RESTORED)					
RTS	(See Fig. 2) RTRN SUB													60	6	1																								—	—	—	—	—	—
SBC	A - M - C̄→A (1)	E9	2	2	ED	4	3	E5	3	2							E1	6	2	F1	5	2	F5	4	2	FD	4	3	F9	4	3									✓	✓	✓ (3)	—	—	✓
SEC	1→C													38	2	1																								—	—	1	—	—	—
SED	1→D													F8	2	1																								—	—	—	—	1	—
SEI	1→I													78	2	1																								—	—	—	1	—	—
STA	A→M				8D	4	3	85	3	2							81	6	2	91	6	2	95	4	2	9D	5	3	99	5	3									—	—	—	—	—	—
STX	X→M				8E	4	3	86	3	2																												96	4	2	—	—	—	—	—	—
STY	Y→M				8C	4	3	84	3	2													94	4	2																—	—	—	—	—	—
TAX	A→X													AA	2	1																								✓	✓	—	—	—	—
TAY	A→Y													A8	2	1																								✓	✓	—	—	—	—
TSX	S→X													BA	2	1																								✓	✓	—	—	—	—
TXA	X→A													8A	2	1																								✓	✓	—	—	—	—
TXS	X→S													9A	2	1																								—	—	—	—	—	—
TYA	Y→A													98	2	1																								✓	✓	—	—	—	—

(1) ADD 1 TO "N" IF PAGE BOUNDARY IS CROSSED
(2) ADD 1 TO "N" IF BRANCH OCCURS TO SAME PAGE; ADD 2 TO "N" IF BRANCH OCCURS TO DIFFERENT PAGE.
(3) CARRY NOT = BORROW
(4) IF IN DECIMAL MODE Z FLAG IS INVALID ACCUMULATOR MUST BE CHECKED FOR ZERO RESULT

X INDEX X
Y INDEX Y
A ACCUMULATOR
M MEMORY PER EFFECTIVE ADDRESS
Ms MEMORY PER STACK POINTER

+ ADD
- SUBTRACT
∧ AND
∨ OR
∀ EXCLUSIVE OR

✓ MODIFIED
— NOT MODIFIED
M7 MEMORY BIT 7
M6 MEMORY BIT 6
N NO. CYCLES
NO. BYTES

205

APPENDIX L

Finally, here is a memory map of the Commodore 64 and then a table containing all the input/output assignments for the Commodore 64 (SID, VIC II, CIA and 6510) and the function that their bits perform.

COMMODORE 64 MEMORY MAP

LABEL	HEX ADDRESS	DECIMAL LOCATION	DESCRIPTION
D6510	0000	0	6510 On-Chip Data-Direction Register
R6510	0001	1	6510 On-Chip Eight-Bit Input/Output Register
	0002	2	Unused
ADRAY1	0003–0004	3–4	Jump Vector: Convert Floating—Integer
ADRAY2	0005–0006	5–6	Jump Vector: Convert Integer—Floating
CHARAC	0007	7	Search Character
ENDCHR	0008	8	Flag: Scan For Quote At End Of String
TRMPOS	0009	9	Screen Column From Last TAB
VERCK	000A	10	Flag: 0 = Load, 1 = Verify
COUNT	000B	11	Input Buffer Pointer/Number Of Subscripts
DIMFLG	000C	12	Flag: Default Array DImension
VALTYP	000D	13	Data Type: $FF = String, $00 = Numeric
INTFLG	000E	14	Data Type: $80 = Integer, $00 = Floating
GARBFL	000F	15	Flag: DATA Scan/LIST Quote/Garbage Coll
SUBFLG	0010	16	Flag: Subscript Reference/User Function Call
INPFLG	0011	17	Flag: $00 = INPUT, $40 = GET, $98 = READ
TANSGN	0012	18	Flag: TAN Sign/Comparison Result
	0013	19	Flag: INPUT Prompt
LINNUM	0014–0015	20–21	Temp: Integer Value
TEMPPT	0016	22	Pointer: Temporary String Stack

LABEL	HEX ADDRESS	DECIMAL LOCATION	DESCRIPTION
LASTPT	0017–0018	23–24	Last Temporary String Address
TEMPST	0019–0021	25–33	Stack For Temporary Strings
INDEX	0022–0025	34–37	Utility Pointer Area
RESHO	0026–002A	38–42	Floating-Point Product Of Multiply
TXTTAB	002B–002C	43–44	Pointer: Start Of BASIC Text
VARTAB	002D–002E	45–46	Pointer: Start Of BASIC Variables
ARYTAB	002F–0030	47–48	Pointer: Start Of BASIC Arrays
STREND	0031–0032	49–50	Pointer: End Of BASIC Arrays (+1)
FRETOP	0033–0034	51–52	Pointer: Bottom Of String Storage
FRESPC	0035–0036	53–54	Utility String Pointer
MEMSIZ	0037–0038	55–56	Pointer: Highest Address Used By BASIC
CURLIN	0039–003A	57–58	Current BASIC Line Number
OLDLIN	003B–003C	59–60	Previous BASIC Line Number
OLDTXT	003D–003E	61–62	Pointer: BASIC Statement For CONT
DATLIN	003F–0040	63–64	Current DATA Line Number
DATPTR	0041–0042	65–66	Pointer: Current DATA Item Address
INPPTR	0043–0044	67–68	Vector: INPUT Routine
VARNAM	0045–0046	69–70	Current BASIC Variable Name
VARPNT	0047–0048	71–72	Pointer: Current BASIC Variable Data
FORPNT	0049–004A	73–74	Pointer: Index Variable For FOR/NEXT
	004B–0060	75–96	Temp Pointer/Data Area
FACEXP	0061	97	Floating-Point Accumulator #1: Exponent
FACHO	0062–0065	98–101	Floating Accumulator. #1: Mantissa
FACSGN	0066	102	Floating Accumulator #1: Sign
SGNFLG	0067	103	Pointer: Series Evaluation Constant
BITS	0068	104	Floating Accumulator #1: Overflow Digit
ARGEXP	0069	105	Floating-Point Accumulator #2: Exponent

LABEL	HEX ADDRESS	DECIMAL LOCATION	DESCRIPTION
ARGHO	006A–006D	106–109	Floating Accumulator #2: Mantissa
ARGSGN	006E	110	Floating Accumulator #2: Sign
ARISGN	006F	111	Sign Comparison Result: Accumulator #1 vs #2
FACOV	0070	112	Floating Accumulator #1. Low-Order (Rounding)
FBUFPT	0071–0072	113–114	Pointer: Cassette Buffer
CHRGET	0073–008A	115–138	Subroutine: Get Next Byte Of BASIC Text
CHRGOT	0079	121	Entry To Get Same Byte Of Text Again
TXTPTR	007A–007B	122–123	Pointer: Current Byte Of Basic Text
RNDX	008B–008F	139–143	Floating RND Function Seed Value
STATUS	0090	144	Kernal I/O Status Word: ST
STKEY	0091	145	Flag: STOP key/RVS key
SVXT	0092	146	Timing Constant For Tape
VERCK	0093	147	Flag: 0 = Load, 1 = Verify
C3PO	0094	148	Flag: Serial Bus—Output Character Buffered
BSOUR	0095	149	Buffered Character For Serial Bus
SYNO	0096	150	Cassette Sync Number
	0097	151	Temporary Data Area
LDTND	0098	152	Number Of Open Files/ Index To File Table
DFLTN	0099	153	Default Input Device (0)
DFLTO	009A	154	Default Output (CMD) Device (3)
PRTY	009B	155	Tape Character Parity
DPSW	009C	156	Flag: Tape Byte-Received
MSGFLG	009D	157	Flag: $80 = Direct Mode, $00 = Program
PTR1	009E	158	Tape Pass 1 Error Log
PTR2	009F	159	Tape Pass 2 Error Log
TIME	00A0–00A2	160–162	Real-Time Jiffy Clock (approx) 1/60th Sec
	00A3–00A4	163–164	Temporary Data Area
CNTDN	00A5	165	Cassette Sync Countdown
BUFPNT	00A6	166	Pointer: Tape I/O Buffer
INBIT	00A7	167	RS-232 Input Bits/Cassette Temp
BITCI	00A8	168	RS-232 Input Bit Count/ Cassette Temp
RINONE	00A9	169	RS-232 Flag: Check For Start Bit

208

LABEL	HEX ADDRESS	DECIMAL LOCATION	DESCRIPTION
RIDATA	00AA	170	RS-232 Input Byte Buffer/Cassette Temp
RIPRTY	00AB	171	RS-232 Input Parity/ Cassette Short Cnt
SAL	00AC–00AD	172–173	Pointer: Tape Buffer/ Screen Scrolling
EAL	00AE–00AF	174–175	Tape End Addresses/End Of Program
CMPO	00B0–00B1	176–177	Tape Timing Constants
TAPE1	00B2–00B3	178–179	Pointer: Start Of Tape Buffer
BITTS	00B4	180	RS-232 Out Bit Count/ Cassette Temp
NXTBIT	00B5	181	RS-232 Next Bit To Send/ Tape EOT Flag
RODATA	00B6	182	RS-232 Out Byte Buffer
FNLEN	00B7	183	Length Of Current File Name
LA	00B8	184	Current Logical File Number
SA	00B9	185	Current Secondary Address
FA	00BA	186	Current Device Number
FNADR	00BB–00BC	187–188	Pointer: Current File Name
ROPRTY	00BD	189	RS-232 Out Parity/ Cassette Temp
FSBLK	00BE	190	Cassette Read/Write Block Count
MYCH	00BF	191	Serial Word Buffer
CAS1	00C0	192	Tape Motor Interlock
STAL	00C1–00C2	193–194	I/O Start Address
MEMUSS	00C3–00C4	195–196	Tape Load Temps
LSTX	00C5	197	Current Key Pressed: CHR$(n) 0 = No Key
NDX	00C6	198	Number Of Characters In Keyboard Buffer (Queue)
RVS	00C7	199	Flag: Print Reverse Characters—1 = Yes, 0 = No Used
INDX	00C8	200	Pointer: End Of Logical Line For INPUT
LXSP	00C9–00CA	201–202	Cursor X-Y Position At Start Of INPUT
SFDX	00CB	203	Flag: Print Shifted Characters
BLNSW	00CC	204	Cursor Blink Enable: 0 = Flash Cursor

LABEL	HEX ADDRESS	DECIMAL LOCATION	DESCRIPTION
BLNCT	00CD	205	Timer: Countdown To Toggle Cursor
GDBLN	00CE	206	Character Under Cursor
BLNON	00CF	207	Flag: Last Cursor Blink On/Off
CRSW	00D0	208	Flag: INPUT Or GET From Keyboard
PNT	00D1–00D2	209–210	Pointer: Current Screen Line Address
PNTR	00D3	211	Cursor Column On Current Line
QTSW	00D4	212	Flag: Editor In Quote Mode, $00 = NO
LNMX	00D5	213	Physical Screen Line Length
TBLX	00D6	214	Current Cursor Physical Line Number
	00D7	215	Temporary Data Area
INSRT	00D8	216	Flag: Insert Mode, >0 = # INSTs
LDTB1	00D9–00F2	217–242	Screen Line Link Table/ Editor Temps
USER	00F3–00F4	243–244	Pointer: Current Screen Colour RAM Location
KEYTAB	00F5–00F6	245–246	Vector: Keyboard Decode Table
RIBUF	00F7–00F8	247–248	RS-232 Input Buffer Pointer
ROBUF	00F9–00FA	249–250	RS-232 Output Buffer Pointer
FREKZP	00FB–00FE	251–254	Free 0-Page Space For User Programs
BASZPT	00FF	255	BASIC Temp Data Area
	0100–01FF	256–511	Microprocessor System Stack Area
	0100–010A	256–266	Floating To String Work Area
BAD	0100–013E	256–318	Tape Input Error Log
BUF	0200–0258	512–600	System INPUT Buffer
LAT	0259–0262	601–610	KERNAL Table: Active Logical File Numbers
FAT	0263–026C	611–620	KERNAL Table: Device Number For Each File
SAT	026D–0276	621–630	KERNAL Table: Second Address Each File
KEYD	0277–0280	631–640	Keyboard Buffer Queue (FIFO)
MEMSTR	0281–0282	641–642	Pointer: Bottom Of Memory For Operating System

LABEL	HEX ADDRESS	DECIMAL LOCATION	DESCRIPTION
MEMSIZ	0283–0284	643–644	Pointer: Top of Memory For Operating System
TIMOUT	0285	645	Flag: Kernal Variable For IEEE Timeout
COLOR	0286	646	Current Character Colour Code
GDCOL	0287	647	Background Colour Under Cursor
HIBASE	0288	648	Top Of Screen Memory (Page)
XMAX	0289	649	Size Of Keyboard Buffer
RPTFLG	028A	650	Flag: REPEAT Key Used, $80 = Repeat
KOUNT	028B	651	Repeat Speed Counter
DELAY	028C	652	Repeat Delay Counter
SHFLAG	028D	653	Flag: Keyboard Shift Key/ CTRL Key/C = Key
LSTSHF	028E	654	Last Keyboard Shift Pattern
KEYLOG	028F–0290	655–656	Vector: Keyboard Table Set-up
MODE	0291	657	Flag: $00 = Disable Shift Keys, $80 = Enable Shift Keys
AUTODN	0292	658	Flag: Auto Scroll Down, 0 = ON
M51CTR	0293	659	RS232: 6551 Control Register Image
M51CDR	0294	660	RS232: 6551 Command Register Image
M51AJB	0295–0296	661–662	RS232 Non-Standard BPS (Time/2-100) USA
RSSTAT	0297	663	RS232: 6551 Status Register Image
BITNUM	0298	664	RS232 Number of Bits Left To Send
BAUDOF	0299–029A	665–666	RS232 Baud Rate: Full Bit Time (μs)
RIDBE	029B	667	RS232 Index To End Of Input Buffer
RIDBS	029C	668	RS232 Start Of Input Buffer (Page)
RODBS	029D	669	RS232 Start Of Output Buffer (Page)
RODBE	029E	670	RS232 Index To End Of Output Buffer
IRQTMP	02F–02A0	671–672	Holds IRQ Vector During Tape I/O

LABEL	HEX ADDRESS	DECIMAL LOCATION	DESCRIPTION
ENABL	02A1	673	RS232 Enables
	02A2	674	TOD Sense During Cassette I/O
	02A3	675	Temporary Storage For Cassette Read
	02A4	676	Temporary D1 IRQ Indicator For Cassette Read
	02A5	677	Temp For Line Index
	02A6	678	PAL/NTSC Flag, 0 = NTSC, 1 = PAL
	02A7–02FF	679–767	Unused
IERROR	0300–0301	768–769	Vector: Print BASIC Error Message
IMAIN	0302–0303	770–771	Vector: BASIC Warm Start
ICRNCH	0304–0305	772–773	Vector: Tokenize BASIC Text
IQPLOP	0306–0307	774–775	Vector: BASIC Text LIST
IGONE	0308–0309	776–777	Vector: BASIC Character Dispatch
IEVAL	030A–030B	778–779	Vector: BASIC Token Evaluation
SAREG	030C	780	Storage for 6502 A Register
SXREG	030D	781	Storage for 6502 X Register
SYREG	030E	782	Storage For 6502 Y Register
SPREG	030F	783	Storage For 6502 SP Register
USRPOK	0310	784	USR Function Jump Instruction (4C)
USRADD	0311–0312	785–786	USR Address Low Byte/ High Byte
	0313	787	Unused
CINV	0314–0315	788–789	Vector: Hardware IRQ Interrupt
CBINV	0316–0317	790–791	Vector: BRK Instruction Interrupt
NMINV	0318–0319	792–793	Vector: Non-Maskable Interrupt
IOPEN	031A–031B	794–795	KERNAL OPEN Routine Vector
ICLOSE	031C–031D	796–797	KERNAL CLOSE Routine Vector
ICHKIN	031E–031F	798–799	KERNAL CHKIN Routine Vector
ICKOUT	0320–0321	800–801	KERNAL CHKOUT Routine Vector
ICLRCH	0322–0323	802–803	KERNAL CLRCHN Routine Vector

LABEL	HEX ADDRESS	DECIMAL LOCATION	DESCRIPTION
IBASIN	0324–0325	804–805	KERNAL CHRIN Routine Vector
IBSOUT	0326–0327	806–807	KERNAL CHROUT Routine Vector
ISTOP	0328–0329	808–809	KERNAL STOP Routine Vector
IGETIN	032A–032B	810–811	KERNAL GETIN Routine Vector
ICLALL	032C–032D	812–813	KERNAL CLALL Routine Vector
USRCMD	032E–032F	814–815	User-Defined Vector
ILOAD	0330–0331	816–817	KERNAL LOAD Routine
ISAVE	0332–0333	818–819	KERNAL SAVE Routine Vector
	0334–033B	820–827	Unused
TBUFFR	033C–03FB	828–1019	Tape I/O Buffer
	03FC–03FF	1020–1023	Unused
VICSCN	0400–07FF	1024–2047	1024 Byte Screen Memory Area
	0400–07E7	1024–2023	Video Matrix: 25 Lines × 40 Columns
	07F8–07FF	2040–2047	Sprite Data Pointers
	0800–9FFF	2048–40959	Normal BASIC Program Space
	8000–9FFF	32768–40959	VSP Cartridge ROM— 8192 Bytes
	A000–BFFF	40960–49151	BASIC ROM—8192 Bytes (or 8K RAM)
	C000–CFFF	49152–53247	RAM—4096 Bytes
	D000–DFFF	53248–57343	Input/Output Devices And Colour RAM Or Character Generator ROM Or RAM—4096 Bytes
	E000–FFFF	57344–65535	KERNAL ROM—8192 Bytes (Or 8K RAM)

COMMODORE 64 INPUT/OUTPUT ASSIGNMENTS

HEX	DECIMAL	BITS	DESCRIPTION
0000	0	7–0	MOS 6510 Data Direction Register (xx101111) Bit=1: Output, Bit=0: Input, x=Don't Care

213

HEX	DECIMAL	BITS	DESCRIPTION
0001	1		MOS 6510 Micro-Processor On-Chip I/O Port
		0	/LORAM Signal (0=Switch BASIC ROM Out)
		1	/HIRAM Signal (0=Switch Kernal ROM Out)
		2	/CHAREN Signal (0=Switch Char. ROM In)
		3	Cassette Data Output Line
		4	Cassette Switch Sense 1 = Switch Closed
		5	Cassette Motor Control 0 = ON, 1 = OFF
		6–7	Undefined
D000–D02E	53248–54271		MOS 6566 VIDEO INTERFACE CONTROLLER (VIC)
D000	53248		Sprite 0 X Position
D001	53249		Sprite 0 Y Position
D002	53250		Sprite 1 X Position
D003	53251		Sprite 1 Y Position
D004	53252		Sprite 2 X Position
D005	53253		Sprite 2 Y Position
D006	53254		Sprite 3 X Position
D007	53255		Sprite 3 Y Position
D008	53256		Sprite 4 X Position
D009	53257		Sprite 4 Y Position
D00A	53258		Sprite 5 X Position
D00B	53259		Sprite 5 Y Position
D00C	53260		Sprite 6 X Position
D00D	53261		Sprite 6 Y Position
D00E	53262		Sprite 7 X Position
D00F	53263		Sprite 7 Y Position
D010	53264		Sprites 0–7 X Position (MSB Of X Co-ordinate)
D011	53265		VIC Control Register
		7	Raster Compare: (Bit 8) See 53266
		6	Extended Colour Text Mode: 1 = Enable
		5	Bit-Map Mode: 1 = Enable
		4	Blank Screen to Border Colour: 0 = Blank
		3	Select 24/25 Row Text Display: 1 = 25 Rows
		2–0	Smooth Scroll To Y Dot-Position (0–7)
D012	53266		Read Raster/Write Raster Value For Compare IRQ
D013	53267		Light-Pen Latch X Position

HEX	DECIMAL	BITS	DESCRIPTION
D014	53268		Light-Pen Latch Y Position
D015	53269		Sprite Display Enable: 1 = Enable
D016	53270		VIC Control Register
		7–6	Unused
		5	ALWAYS SET THIS BIT TO 0!
		4	Multi-Colour Mode: 1 = Enable (Text Or Bit-Map)
		3	Select 38/40 Column Text Display: 1 = 40 Cols
		2–0	Smooth Scroll To X Position
D017	53271		Sprites 0–7 Expand 2× Vertical (Y)
D018	53272		VIC Memory Control Register
		7–4	Video Matrix Base Address (Inside VIC)
		3–1	Character Dot-Data Base Address (Inside VIC)
D019	53273		VIC Interrupt Flag Register (Bit = 1: IRQ Occurred)
		7	Set On Any Enabled VIC IRQ Condition
		3	Light-Pen Triggered IRQ Flag
		2	Sprite To Sprite Collision IRQ Flag
		1	Sprite To Background Collision IRQ Flag
		0	Raster Compare IRQ Flag
D01A	53274		IRQ Mask Register: 1 = Interrupt Enabled
DO1B	53275		Sprite To Background Display Priority: 1 = Sprite
D01C	53276		Sprites 0–7 Multi-Colour Mode Select: 1 = M.C.M.
D01D	53277		Sprites 0–7 Expand 2 × Horizontal (X)
D01E	53278		Sprite To Sprite Collision Detect
D01F	53279		Sprite To Background Collision Detect
D020	53280		Border Colour
D021	53281		Background Colour 0
D022	53282		Background Colour 1
D023	53283		Background Colour 2
D024	53284		Background Colour 3

HEX	DECIMAL	BITS	DESCRIPTION
D025	53285		Sprite Multi-Colour Register 0
D026	53286		Sprite Multi-Colour Register 1
D027	53287		Sprite 0 Colour
D028	53288		Sprite 1 Colour
D029	53289		Sprite 2 Colour
D02A	53290		Sprite 3 Colour
D02B	53291		Sprite 4 Colour
D02C	53292		Sprite 5 Colour
D02D	53293		Sprite 6 Colour
D02E	53294		Sprite 7 Colour
D400–D7FF	54272–55295		MOS 6581 SOUND INTERFACE DEVICE (SID)
D400	54272		Voice 1: Frequency Control—Low-Byte
D401	54273		Voice 1: Frequency Control—High-Byte
D402	54274		Voice 1: Pulse Waveform Width—Low-Byte
D403	54275	7–4	Unused
		3–0	Voice 1: Pulse Waveform Width—High-Nybble
D404	54276		Voice 1: Control Register
		7	Select Random Noise Waveform, 1 = On
		6	Select Pulse Waveform, 1 = On
		5	Select Sawtooth Waveform, 1 = On
		4	Select Triangle Waveform, 1 = On
		3	Test Bit: 1 = Disable Oscillator 1
		2	Ring Modulate Oscillator, 1 With Oscillator 3 Output, 1 = On
		1	Synchronize Oscillator, 1 With Oscillator 3 Frequency, 1 = On
		0	Gate Bit: 1 = Start Attack/Decay/Sustain, 0 = Start Release

HEX	DECIMAL	BITS	DESCRIPTION
D405	54277		Envelope Generator 1: Attack/Decay Cycle Control
		7–4	Select Attack Cycle Duration: 0–15
		3–0	Select Decay Cycle Duration: 0–15
D406	54278		Envelope Generator 1: Sustain/Release Cycle Control
		7–4	Select Sustain Cycle Duration: 0–15
		3–0	Select Release Cycle Duration: 0–15
D407	54279		Voice 2: Frequency Control—Low-Byte
D408	54280		Voice 2: Frequency Control—High-Byte
D409	54281		Voice 2: Pulse Waveform Width—Low-Byte
D40A	54282	7–4	Unused
		3–0	Voice 2: Pulse Waveform Width—High-Nybble
D40B	54283		Voice 2: Control Register
		7	Select Random Noise Waveform, 1 = On
		6	Select Pulse Waveform, 1 = On
		5	Select Sawtooth Waveform, 1 = On
		4	Select Triangle Waveform, 1 = On
		3	Test Bit: 1 = Disable Oscillator 2
		2	Ring Modulate Oscillator 2 with Oscillator 1 Output, 1 = On
		1	Synchronize Oscillator 2 with Oscillator 1 Frequency, 1 = On
		0	Gate Bit: 1 = Start Attack/Decay/Sustain, 0 = Start Release
D40C	54284		Envelope Generator 2: Attack/Decay Cycle Control
		7–4	Select Attack Cycle Duration: 0–15
		3–0	Select Decay Cycle Duration: 0–15

HEX	DECIMAL	BITS	DESCRIPTION
D40D	54285		Envelope Generator 2: Sustain/Release Cycle Control
		7–4	Select Sustain Cycle Duration: 0–15
		3–0	Select Release Cycle Duration: 0–15
D40E	54286		Voice 3: Frequency Control—Low-Byte
D40F	54287		Voice 3: Frequency Control—High-Byte
D410	54288		Voice 3: Pulse Waveform Width—Low-Byte
D411	54289	7–4	Unused
		3–0	Voice 3: Pulse Waveform Width—High-Nybble
D412	54290		Voice 3: Control Register
		7	Select Random Noise Waveform, 1 = On
		6	Select Pulse Waveform, 1 = On
		5	Select Sawtooth Waveform, 1 = On
		4	Select Triangle Waveform, 1 = On
		3	Test Bit: 1 = Disable Oscillator 3
		2	Ring Modulate Oscillator 3 with Oscillator 2 Output, 1 = On
		1	Synchronize Oscillator 3 with Oscillator 2 Frequency, 1 = On
		0	Gate Bit: 1 = Start Attack/Decay/Sustain, 0 = Start Release
D413	54291		Envelope Generator 3: Attack/Decay Cycle Control
		7–4	Select Attack Cycle Duration: 0–15
		3–0	Select Decay Cycle Duration: 0–15
D414	54292		Envelope Generator 3: Sustain/Release Cycle Control
		7–4	Select Sustain Cycle Duration: 0–15
		3–0	Select Release Cycle Duration: 0–15

HEX	DECIMAL	BITS	DESCRIPTION
D415	54293		Filter Cut-off Frequency: Low-Nybble (Bits 2-0)
D416	54294		Filter Cut-Off Frequency: High-Byte
D417	54295		Filter Resonance Control/ Voice Input Control
		7-4	Select Filter Resonance: 0-15
		3	Filter External Input: 1 = Yes, 0 = No
		2	Filter Voice 3 Output: 1 = Yes, 0 = No
		1	Filter Voice 2 Output: 1 = Yes, 0 = No
		0	Filter Voice 1 Output: 1 = Yes, 0 = No
D418	54296		Select Filter Mode And Volume
		7	Cut-Off Voice 3 Output: 1 = Off, 0 = On
		6	Select Filter high-Pass Mode: 1 = On
		5	Select Filter Band-Pass Mode: 1 = On
		4	Select Filter Low-Pass Mode: 1 = On
		3-0	Select Output Volume: 0-15
D419	54297		Analog/Digital Converter: Game Paddle 1 (0-255)
D41A	54298		Analog/Digital Converter: Game Paddle 2 (0-255)
D41B	54299		Oscillator 3 Random Number Generator
D41C	54230		Envelope Generator 3 Output
D500-D7FF	54528-55295		SID IMAGES
D800-DBFF	55296-56319		Colour RAM (Nybbles)
DC00-DCFF	56320-56575		MOS 6526 Complex Interface Adapter (CIA) #1
DC00	56320		Data Port A (Keyboard, Joystick, Paddles, Light-Pen)
		7-0	Write Keyboard Column Values For Keyboard Scan
		7-6	Read Paddles On Port A/ B (01 = Port A, 10 = Port B)

219

HEX	DECIMAL	BITS	DESCRIPTION
		4	Joystick A Fire Button: 1 = Fire
		3–2	Paddle Fire Buttons
		3–0	Joystick A Direction (0–15)
DC01	56321		Data Port B (Keyboard, Joystick, Paddles): Game Port 1
		7–0	Read Keyboard Row Values For Keyboard Scan
		7	Timer B: Toggle/Pulse Output
		6	Timer A: Toggle/Pulse Output
		4	Joystick 1 Fire Button: 1 = Fire
		3–2	Paddle Fire Buttons
		3–0	Joystick 1 Direction
DC02	56322		Data Direction Register—Port A (56320)
DC03	56323		Data Direction Register—Port B (56321)
DC04	56324		Timer A: Low-Byte
DC05	56325		Timer A: High-Byte
DC06	56326		Timer B: Low-Byte
DC07	56327		Timer B: High-Byte
DC08	56328		Time-Of Day Clock: 1/10 Seconds
DC09	56329		Time-Of-Day Clock: Seconds
DC0A	56330		Time-Of-Day Clock: Minutes
DC08	56331		Time-Of-Day Clock: Hours + AM/PM Flag (Bit 7)
DC0C	56332		Synchronous Serial I/O Data Buffer
DC0D	56333		CIA Interrupt Control Register (Read IRQs/ Write Mask)
		7	IRQ Flag (1 = IRQ Occurred)/Set-Clear Flag
		4	FLAG1 IRQ (Cassette Read/Serial Bus SRQ Input)
		3	Serial Port Interrupt
		2	Time-Of-Day Clock Alarm Interrupt
		1	Timer B Interrupt
		0	Timer A Interrupt

HEX	DECIMAL	BITS	DESCRIPTION
DCOE	56334		CIA Control Register A
		7	Time-Of-Day Clock Frequency: 1 = 50 Hz, 0 = 60 Hz
		6	Serial Port I/O Mode: 1 = output, 0 = input
		5	Timer A Counts: 1 = CNT Signals, 0 = System 02 Clock
		4	Force Load Timer A: 1 = Yes
		3	Timer A Run Mode: 1 = One-Shot, 0 = Continuous
		2	Timer A Output Mode To PB6: 1 = Toggle, 0 = Pulse
		1	Timer A Output On PB6: 1 = Yes, 0 = No
		0	Start/Stop Timer A: 1 = Start, 0 = Stop
DC0F	56335		CIA Control Register B
		7	Set Alarm/TOD-Clock: 1 = Alarm, 0 = Clock
		6–5	Timer B Mode Select: 00 = Count System 02 Clock Pulses 01 = Count Positive CNT Transitions 10 = Count Timer A Underflow Pulses 11 = Count Timer A Underflows While CNT Positive
		4–0	Same As CIA Control Register A—for Timer B
DD00–DDFF	56576–56831		MOS 6526 Complex Interface Adapter (CIA) #2
DD00	56576		Data Port A (Serial Bus, RS232, VIC Memory Control)
		7	Serial Bus Data Input
		6	Serial Bus Clock Pulse Input
		5	Serial Bus Data Output
		4	Serial Bus Clock Pulse Output
		3	Serial Bus ATN Signal Output
		2	RS232 Data Output (User Port)

221

HEX	DECIMAL	BITS	DESCRIPTION
		1–0	VIC Chip System Memory Bank Select (Default = 11)
DD01	56577		Data Port B (User Port, RS232)
		7	User/RS232 Data Set Ready
		6	User/RS232 Clear To Send
		5	User
		4	User/RS232 Carrier Detect
		3	User/RS232 Ring Indicator
		2	User/RS232 Data Terminal Ready
		1	User/RS232 Request To Send
		0	User/RS232 Received Data
DD02	56578		Data Direction Register—Port A
DD03	56579		Data Direction Register—Part B
DD04	56580		Timer A: Low-Byte
DD05	56581		Timer A: High-Byte
DD06	56582		Timer B: Low-Byte
DD07	56583		Timer B: High-Byte
DD08	56584		Time-Of-Day Clock: 1/10 Seconds
DD09	56585		Time-Of-Day Clock: Seconds
DD0A	56586		Time-Of-Day Clock: Minutes
DD0B	56587		Time-Of-Day Clock: Hours + AM/PM Flag (Bit 7)
DD0C	56588		Synchronous Serial I/O Data Buffer
DD0D	56589		CIA Interrupt Control Register (Read NMIs/ Write Mask)
		7	NMI Flag (1 = NMI Occurred)/Set-Clear Flag
		4	FLAG1 NMI (User/RS232 Received Data Input)
		3	Serial Port Interrupt
		1	Timer B Interrupt
		0	Timer A Interrupt

HEX	DECIMAL	BITS	DESCRIPTION
DD0E	56590		CIA Control Register A
		7	Time-Of-Day Clock Frequency: 1 = 50 Hz, 0 = 60 Hz
		6	Serial Port I/O Mode: 1 = Output, 0 = Input
		5	Timer A Counts: 1 = CNT Signals, 0 = System 02 Clock
		4	Force Load Timer A: 1 = Yes
		3	Timer A Run Mode: 1 = One-Shot, 0 = Con-tinuous
		2	Timer A Output Mode to PB6: 1 = Toggle, 0 = Pulse
		1	Timer A Output on PB6: 1 = Yes, 0 = No
		0	Start/Stop Timer A: 1 = Start, 0 = Stop
DD0F	56591		CIA Control Register B
		7	Set Alarm/TOD-Clock: 1 = Alarm, 0 = Clock
		6–5	Timer B Mode Select: 00 = Count System 02 Clock Pulses 01 = Count Positive CNT Transitions 10 = Count Timer A Underflow Pulses 11 = Count Timer A Underflows While CNT Positive
		4–0	Same As CIA Control Register A—For Timer B
DE00–DEFF	56832–57087		Reserved For Future I/O Expansion
DF00–DFFF	57088–57343		Reserved For Future I/O Expansion

INDEX FOR MASTERING MACHINE CODE ON YOUR COMMODORE 64

NOTES

Mastering the Commodore 64

Mark Greenshields

www.ingramcontent.com/pod-product-compliance
Lightning Source LLC
LaVergne TN
LVHW041204050326
832903LV00020B/442